D0777021

ADVANCE PRAISE

"The ability to consistently hire the right people is the difference between building a truly great company and just a good one. This book is the how-to manual for doing exactly that. It will save you hundreds of hours of trying to figure it out yourself. I'm recommending it to all of our clients."

—GINO WICKMAN, author of *Traction* and creator of EOS

"Hiring the right senior executives is critical to the success of a fast-growing enterprise. Top talent attracts top talent and separates the best startups from the rest of the pack. If you dream of starting or growing a business, this is an essential book to learn how to execute the most important roles of a leader—recruiting and creating the culture."

—JULES MALTZ, General Partner, IVP

"Too many companies hire without a blueprint. However, 'winging it' and making such important decisions with your 'gut' is a recipe for disaster. Dave Carvajal provides a thoughtful guidebook for making one of the most critical decisions a company can make—getting the right people on board."

—NIR EYAL, bestselling author of *Hooked: How to Build Habit-Forming Products*

"Dave Carvajal is a proven luminary in talent and team development. His *Hire Smart from the Start* is a go-to roadmap for any company seeking to build a team that contributes to fostering strong culture, evangelizing the broader business, and delivering results."

—JOHN FRANKEL, founding partner of ff Venture Capital

"After 25 years of venture capital investing and supporting entrepreneurs, this is what I know for certain: If you hire wrong—you lose time and money. This is a 'learned art,' so it helps to have a Sherpa like Dave Carvajal guide you through the mountain pass."

—JEANNE M. SULLIVAN, co-founder of StarVest Partners

"This is a well-written, useful, and practical guide for all leaders who aspire to grow their businesses. By making recruiting and culture their competitive strategic advantage, entrepreneurs and seasoned leaders can implement the lessons and process in *Hire Smart from the Start* to compete, recruit, and secure the greatest talent."

—NICK BEIM, Partner, Venrock

"Dave Carvajal is exceptional at understanding how to recruit teams (players) that embrace and embody a company's vision, toward creating high-performance teams. *Hire Smart from the Start* lays the groundwork for achieving your mission with the right values and people."

—JULIE ALLEGRO, founder and Managing Director, FYRFLY Venture Partners, and founder and Co-Chair, V Foundation Wine Celebration

"A leading company is more than a well-differentiated product with a brilliant strategy. Success comes from strong leadership and a highly talented team. This book provides all the right principles to ensure that your company achieves ultimate success through your most valuable resource: people."

—PAUL CAINE, founder, PC Ventures, LLC; Executive Chairman of the Board of Telaria (formerly Tremor Video); former Global Chief Revenue & Client Partnerships Officer of Bloomberg

HIRE SMART FROM THE START

The Entrepreneur's Guide to Finding, Catching, and Keeping the Best Talent for Your Company

DAVE CARVAJAL

AMACOM

AMERICAN MANAGEMENT ASSOCIATION

New York • Atlanta • Brussels • Chicago • Mexico City • San Francisco
Shanghai • Tokyo • Toronto • Washington, D.C.

This publication is designed to provide accurate and authoritative information in regard to the subject matter covered. It is sold with the understanding that the publisher is not engaged in rendering legal, accounting, or other professional service. If legal advice or other expert assistance is required, the services of a competent professional person should be sought.

Library of Congress Cataloging-in-Publication Data

Names: Carvajal, Dave, author.
Title: Hire smart from the start : the entrepreneur's guide to finding,
    catching, and keeping the best talent for your company / Dave Carvajal.
Description: New York : AMACOM, [2018] | Includes index.
Identifiers: LCCN 2017030593 (print) | LCCN 2017040988 (ebook) | ISBN
    9780814438275 (ebook) | ISBN 9780814438268 (hardcover)
Subjects: LCSH: Employee selection. | Employee retention. | Personnel
    management.
Classification: LCC HF5549.5.S38 (ebook) | LCC HF5549.5.S38 C375 2018 (print)
    | DDC 658.3/11—dc23
LC record available at https://lccn.loc.gov/2017030593

About AMA
American Management Association (www.amanet.org) is a world leader in talent development, advancing the skills of individuals to drive business success. Our mission is to support the goals of individuals and organizations through a complete range of products and services, including classroom and virtual seminars, webcasts, webinars, podcasts, conferences, corporate and government solutions, business books, and research. AMA's approach to improving performance combines experiential learning—learning through doing—with opportunities for ongoing professional growth at every step of one's career journey.

10 9 8 7 6 5 4 3 2 1

CONTENTS

Acknowledgments   **vii**

Foreword   **ix**

Introduction   **1**

1   New Rules for a New Age   **11**

2   Slow Down, Use a Process, Move Beyond the Specs   **29**

3   Recruiting Myths and Realities   **51**

4   Evangelical Zeal and a SEAL Team's Focus   **67**

5   Map the Organization's Foundational Mission and Values   **87**

6   Seeing Your Perceptions and Their Realities   **105**

7   Drivers: *Mapping the Candidates' Missions and Values*   **129**

8   Extract the Matches   **149**

9   High-Level Hires: *Leaders and Managers*   **165**

10   Finding and Recruiting People Who Get Things Done   **185**

11   Your First Hire: *Bringing Entrepreneurial Energy and Agility to a New Skill Set*   **199**

12   The Employee of the Future: *Recruiting with an Eye Toward Emerging Trends*   **217**

Index   **231**

ACKNOWLEDGMENTS

THIS BOOK WAS BORN when AMACOM's Stephen Power showed great faith in me and my subject. So thanks to Stephen, as well as to AMACOM's Ellen Kadin for her compassion and editorial insight and to her entire team of power rangers without whom this book would not be possible.

For his patience, courage to both listen and argue without judgment, and his mastery of the craft I would also like to thank Bruce Wexler.

The more I learn, the more I realize I have yet to learn and am so eternally appreciative of the entire list of mentors, coaches, clients, friends, and top 1% of A+ executive leaders all of whom remind me every single day that in business and in life, leadership and love are the highest calling for the life that is inside of us. This list includes but is not limited to Tony Robbins, Keith Cunningham, Richard Johnson, Martin Babinec, Thilo Semmelbauer, Mary Lou Song, Aditi Javeri Gokhale, Irv Grousbeck, Liza Landsman, Peter Diamandis, Joe Williams, and Dan Sullivan.

To Barb, Liam, Ryan, and Clover: For your encouragement, support, occasional earful, and most of all for endowing me with the richness of all that is beautiful in life, I am grateful.

And, of course, for the divine intelligence that connects us all, I am so grateful.

FOREWORD

WHEN DAVE CARVAJAL TALKS about recruiting for more than just "technical chops," he reminds me how I've tried to look beyond the job specs. While spending nearly a decade as an executive at Microsoft and later as the founder of the not-for-profit, Room to Read, I've searched for candidates who were passionate about what we were trying to accomplish. This was my sine qua non for filling any job.

Obviously, the two organizations are quite different: Microsoft a titan of the technology world, and Room to Read, a little-known startup promoting literacy and gender equality across the developing world. Yet despite the differences in purpose and size, I recruited the same type of people for both—people who communicated their zeal for and excitement about our goals.

Were Microsoft candidates amped up about building a great technology company? Were Room to Read candidates juiced about educating kids and helping millions of children who had lost "the lottery of life" and risked never gaining even a basic education? Who were vulnerable to being caught up in terrorism, human trafficking, and other horrors if they were denied access to education?

I needed to see that spark in their eyes and hear the enthusiasm and commitment in their voices. If I saw it and heard it, they were as good as hired. If they lacked it, it didn't matter how skilled they were; they weren't going to receive a job offer from me.

When Dave writes about the benefits of recruiting people whose mission mirrors that of the founder(s) and whose values fit the culture, I know exactly what he's talking about.

For entrepreneurs, be they startup or not-for-profit founders, overcoming obstacles is crucial for success. The obstacles can run the gamut—competing against better-known not-for-profits for donations or convincing a prospective customer to give you their business rather than a bigger competitor. I've found that when I didn't hire people whose passion and gumption resembled my own, they struggled to overcome obstacles. They gave up, or settled for compromises.

But when they were as stubborn and committed as I was, they found ways to hurdle obstacles—or barrel right through them—in order to reach an objective.

That's why I listen for very specific stories from job candidates. It might be a story about how education helped their grandmother break free from the poverty cycle. Or how when they were a kid, they walked into the school library and the books they discovered were a portal to the world that changed their lives. Or how a teacher helped them achieve something they thought was impossible.

Whatever it is, if I don't hear examples of passion and enthusiasm during the first ten minutes of an interview, my mind starts to drift and I won't hire them.

As I read *Hire Smart from the Start*, I was particularly impressed with Dave's advice about the need for a structured recruiting process—and the process that he details. Dave is someone who has used this process countless times to recruit people for jobs in the hotly competitive tech sector. He's been able to convince leaders to leave great jobs at huge companies for positions at startups.

How? By following the process steps rather than winging it. By definition, entrepreneurs like to fly by the seat of their pants (I'm guilty as charged!). This works in some areas, but it can be a problem in recruiting. For instance, as you may imagine, I tend to respond instinctively when I interview job candidates. If I really like someone, I tell my people, "Hire them, they'll be great." When they ask me why I believe they'll perform well, I respond, "I'm not sure, but just bring them in, let's let them prove how good they can be."

I do not recommend this approach, since it leads to mistakes. And hiring mistakes are costly—especially when you only have a handful of employees. As one of my mentors told me, "People problems tend to age more like milk than wine." If you have four good employees and you hire an ill-fitting fifth one, 20% of your workforce has gone bad.

Entrepreneurs in both the not-for-profit and private sectors can't afford these errors. As Room to Read started to grow (to 1400 employees as of this writing), our team recommended that we implement a more structured process in which they would do the initial round of interviews, asking all those technical questions I'd be less likely to ask. If the candidate made it through those rounds, I could then act as the "closer," assessing for cultural fit, passion, work ethic, and commitment to our cause.

Before we had implemented this structured recruitment and interview approach, we hired some people who were dead wrong for our organization. My Room to Read co-founder Erin and I had been advised that, given our corporate backgrounds, we needed to make sure our next hire was a veteran non-profit professional. This went against our beliefs—we wanted to hire a superstar corporate salesperson to spearhead our fundraising efforts. But board members and others advised us to look in the non-profit world, and we eventually found someone I'll call Kate. She had great credentials, but on her first day, second hour on the job, she loudly announced to the "bullpen" where all five members of our proud little staff were working cheek-to-jowl: "I have a question."

"Fire away," I said.

"What's the company's sick leave policy?"

WTF? was the first thing that came to mind. She's been here for two hours, and this is what's top of her mind? I tried to avoid smiling at the eye rolls of my co-worker Emily, and instead tersely replied: "If you're sick, don't come to work. Otherwise, be here."

I was furious, not just with Kate but with myself. There's nothing wrong with asking about company sick leave at some point. But to make it the first question asked of the boss on the first day of work was a red flag. It demonstrated that she had other things on her mind besides helping our fledging not-for-profit to grow and help as many kids as possible.

I had made this mistake because I hadn't done what Dave advocates: Communicate the company mission and values in a way that provokes an insightful response from job candidates.

From that moment on, I followed Dave's advice.

I didn't mince words during interviews, insisting that we only wanted employees who possessed a Get Shit Done attitude. We told candidates early in the process: "This is not a 9-to-5, Monday-through-Friday kind of place. We're going big, so we'll be delegating a lot to you. If you don't have a strong work ethic, this is not the right company for you."

And most important of all, I described our highly ambitious vision and mission. As I had learned from Microsoft's Bill Gates and Steve Ballmer, bold goals attract bold people. The corollary is also true: wimpy goals attract wimpy people. I sold the big vision—that we'd reach 10 million children with the lifelong gift of education by 2020, and anything less than that was unacceptable. Similarly, I was clear that we were pursuing meteoric growth for the sake of those kids—ultimately, you report to them!

Once I learned how to recruit the right way, we began hiring people who fit with Room to Read and helped our organization to soar. As a result, we reached our 10 millionth student five years early—by 2015, and have raised our 2020 goal to 15 million.

If you want your entrepreneurial enterprise to soar, I highly recommend that you and your entire team read this book. No entrepreneurial journey is ever easy, but if you take Dave's advice to heart, and then implement it, you're a giant step closer to building the world's next great organization. I wish you luck!

—John Wood
Founder of Room to Read

JOHN WOOD is the author of *Leaving Microsoft to Change the World*, which was chosen by Amazon as one of the Top Ten Business Narratives of 2006 and featured on *The Oprah Winfrey Show*. His next book is *The Purpose Migration*.

HIRE SMART FROM THE START

Introduction

Entrepreneurs trust their guts, but if they *only* rely on their instincts when they're hiring, they're bound to make huge mistakes. The rules of recruiting have changed, and one of the changes is the need for a structured, strategic process to complement their guts.

As psychologist Daniel Kahneman points out in his book, *Thinking Fast and Slow*, we often make mistakes when we rely on our fast mode of thinking—instinctive, emotional, and immediate—rather than drawing on slow cognitive processes which are logical and deliberate. Or, as I just noted, structured and strategic.

It used to be that entrepreneurs had greater margins for error—for making these types of hiring mistakes. In the "old" days—before the startup boom in the first decade of the twenty-first century—company founders might hire by the seat of their pants and get away with it. Some of the time, they'd hire the right people. It was like the frequently cited statistic on marriages: 50 percent work, 50 percent fail. But this was an acceptable success/failure percentage. If someone didn't work out, there were plenty of other good candidates to take her place. Besides, even if they ended up hiring someone who was mediocre or even barely competent, the company could survive. If the entrepreneurial enterprise was built on a strong idea or product and had sufficient capital, it could absorb a lack of productivity from some employees.

Today, the margin for error is rapidly approaching zero. Many entrepreneurs have good ideas and sufficient capital. But people have become the new competitive advantage: Without the right people in key positions, one mistake can be devastating. This is especially true in entrepreneurial companies where the ability to get things done—to get them done with speed, creativity, and commitment—is crucial. If someone isn't executing effectively, the company will lose out to a competitor that is.

Entrepreneurs whose businesses excel understand the new rules and priorities of recruiting. For instance, they hire for more than job competence. Obviously, they want people who possess the skills necessary to do a job well. But they also recognize that hiring the most highly skilled individual is worthless in an age where job mobility is at an all-time high; nor does hiring a highly skilled person mean much if she isn't committed heart and soul to the enterprise's mission. Thus, they recruit with a broader, deeper purpose than entrepreneurs in the past.

I'm writing this book to help you with this broader, deeper purpose. Whether you're running a 10-employee restaurant or a 1000-employee tech company, your business depends on learning that the old mindset of recruiting—that it is important but not vital, and that mistakes are not fatal—is obsolete. In this book, you'll learn to:

- Prioritize people over technology/ideas and capital
- Reframe your recruiting mindset to custom-fit talent to your organization (rather than settling for skill competence)
- Use a tried-and-true process to search for individuals whose values/work-styles are compatible with your organization's culture

Throughout the book, I'm going to be referring to mission and values, purpose and beliefs. As an entrepreneur, you were driven to create your company for a reason—you wanted to be a disruptive innovator, to make the world a better place, to become a leader in your field. Similarly, you possess certain beliefs about work that you've instilled in your organization's culture—honesty, loyalty, transparency.

Though I'm going to use different words to describe these drivers and how they manifest themselves, the key is finding compatibility between a candidate's purpose and values and those of your company.

Approaching recruitment with a new mindset and new priorities can be challenging. I'll help you meet this challenge in the following pages, but first, I'd like to give you a sense of how I developed my understanding of and ability to capitalize on the new recruiting paradigm.

When I started working for a top executive search firm in New York City, I was in my twenties and possessed the time and motivation to outwork everyone else. Back then I was learning on the job and I didn't have a particularly sophisticated concept of what executive search was. But I discovered that if I put in a lot of hours, I could usually fill positions with qualified people.

It was only when I left this large search firm and helped start HotJobs.com that I began gaining insight into what recruiting was all about—and how the business was changing to reflect a changing business environment. Startups were becoming hot, as was the demand for people to work at them. As co-founder of HotJobs, I built it into a company with 650 employees and $1.2 billion in market capitalization and along the way began changing my recruiting approach dramatically. My epiphany was that it wasn't just about meeting the job specs; it was about matching candidates' work preferences and values to those of a given company and culture. This required organizational self-awareness and an objective view of who candidates were—their expertise as well as their values and work personas. Instead of just filling a vacancy for the short term, this would create tremendous long-term value for a company.

By 2008, I built Ladders.com into one of the hottest startups in New York City and evolved my methods further. At Ladders (and subsequently when I launched Dave Partners, a specialized recruitment firm), I developed a method to "extract and secure" the best and the brightest. In almost every instance, the right person for the job already had an excellent position with an excellent company. How could you pry these individuals out of seemingly ideal situations and induce them to accept a new position? That's the challenge of what I call "extracting."

My methodology is designed for an era where people are more important to a company's success than ever before; where the best prospective employees won't leave their current employers unless they resonate personally to a company's culture and mission; and where lots of people are qualified for a given job but only a handful are going to provide major long-term value.

Though I've applied this methodology primarily for high-growth startups in the tech sector, it is designed for an entrepreneurial company of any size and type. The only three criteria are:

1. Your company rises or falls based on the ability of your people to get the job done, quickly, effectively, and creatively.
2. You possess a distinctive culture and mission, and that the people you hire perform better and longer when their values mirror that culture and mission.
3. You run your company like a business and not a ma-and-pa corner store.

This last criterion needs a little explanation. Some people are content to run small companies that don't grow much or that deliver marginal profits. They are happy to scrape by year after year. Some do better than scrape by, but they have no growth strategy in place; they are content to do well but aren't driven to do better.

I'm not making a judgment, but I am raising a warning flag if the previous description fits you. The methodology I'm presenting is for entrepreneurs who have a vision for what their companies might become, who dream of growing them and making a greater impact in their fields. While I think you can still learn a lot from this book about how to hire the right person, you may not want to invest the time and energy in using these methods if you're content to maintain your business rather than grow it.

The methodology to which I've been referring will be explained and illustrated throughout the book, but for now, think about it in the context of recruiting "levels."

Level 1 recruiting involves Internet advertising—you run an ad on a jobs site and are inundated with responses from applicants, many of whom lack the requisite skills or experience for the job. Finding the right one is a search for the proverbial needle in a haystack; the high volume of responses makes it difficult to find well-qualified applicants. This is an especially poor approach if you're looking to fill a job with a significant amount of responsibility.

Level 2 recruiting is when you're relying on "referrals and networking." If you hire a big search firm, they will try to get you candidates quickly by using large-scale referrals and networking. They will present a list of people who are what I refer to as "available and convenient." It's the modern equivalent of the old boy's network or even nepotism—someone knows someone and that's why they're being put forward as a candidate. While they may have the right background for the job, they often are a poor fit. They may be available and convenient because they don't play well with others . . . or because they're lazy . . . or because they're lame ducks who just want to put in their time and retire. Even if you don't use a search firm, you can still do Level 2 recruiting on your own by asking colleagues if they know of anyone who might be available, qualified, and interested in your opening. Again, you're being reactive—depending on what's available and convenient rather than being proactive and searching for someone who is tailor-made for the position.

Level 3 recruiting is what this book is about. It's about extracting and securing the highest caliber talent. It's about identifying who are the best 10 or 100 people on the planet—whatever it takes—to fill the position. It is about going through that list and identifying who is the best candidate FOR US. I put these words in capital letters because FOR US changes everything. Does this individual's DNA match the cultural DNA of the CEO? Does this person's vision of where he wants to be align with where the organization is heading?

The methodology that I'll share is built around this high-level approach to recruiting, and in the following pages you'll find all sorts of tools to help you find these incredibly productive, incredibly well-fitting people, whether you're searching for a new CEO for your fast-growing tech company or a foreman for your plant.

I should also tell you that this book operates on two distinct and highly optimistic premises: First, that there is an A+ player for every role in every company. And second, that everyone is a potential recruit under the right set of circumstances. I believe an abundance of talent exists in every entrepreneurial business. I've been involved in recruiting for over twenty years, and I've never seen so many talented people at all levels.

But to take advantage of this talent, you may need to shift your philosophy about what makes a business successful. Since the beginning of time, when humans began to organize around commercial enterprise, the ingredients for outrageous entrepreneurial success have been the same: people, ideas, capital. Today, there is more money available than ever before to entrepreneurs (through venture capital, angel investors, Kickstarter and other social media campaigns, and so on). Ideas, too, are plentiful, due in no small part to the Internet and the way in which it has democratized knowledge, facilitating research, exchanges of information, and brainstorming. Good ideas have become the ante to get in the game.

What helps you win the game—and keep winning it year after year—are people. In our knowledge economy, the value of the best people (over the merely competent) will have an exponential impact on your team, your company, and your results. In any sector where the pace of innovation is accelerating—the tech arena especially—speed in execution is crucial. And people are responsible for execution. The better the fit between people and organizations, the faster and better they get things done.

The book is divided into three sections. The first focuses on why a new set of rules for twenty-first century recruiting has emerged and why it's imperative for entrepreneurs to understand them and recruit with these new rules in mind. The second section describes the four-step process for implementing Level 3 recruiting, offering graphics, checklists, and other tools. The third section focuses on specific challenges, such as hiring leaders, hiring people who can get things done, and learning to become an effective recruiter when you've never done it before. The book ends with a chapter on recruiting the employee of the future.

In all these sections, I'll provide examples—both cautionary tales and inspiring stories. For instance, Nancy was the number three person at one of the world's largest and most successful companies. She had a terrific leadership position and was greatly appreciated by her company. About a year ago, a startup founder, Charles, came to our firm and was looking to hire a CEO. Charles talked about his vision for the startup—the highly ambitious growth strategy, the desire to create a company that did well but also did good in the world, the culture of inclusion and equality—and the more he talked, the more I realized that this would be a difficult position to fill.

Charles needed someone who was driven and was up for a major challenge. He also needed someone who had experience taking a small company and orchestrating a rapid growth strategy. And he needed someone who was comfortable working in an environment where people didn't have position power but were able to wield influence based on their ability to manage a variety of teams.

We began the recruitment process and turned up a number of qualified candidates, but most of them had never taken a startup from A to Z in record time. When I came across Nancy, though, I could see that potentially, she was the one. Beyond the fact that she possessed the right expertise and experience, she was perfect for the startup's culture. Even though her personality was very different from Charles, her values and vision were remarkably similar to those of the startup founder. The question, of course, was whether she would leave a top job with a top global company to run a startup.

The answer turned out to be yes. When she met with Charles and heard about his short-term and long-term goals, she said it was like she was talking to a spiritual business brother. She knew that even though it was a step down in one sense, it was a step up in a larger sense. Nancy accepted the position, and almost from her first day on the job, she's been growing the startup like crazy.

This book will help you find and recruit your own "Nancys" and provide a wide variety of benefits in the process, including:

- The ability to make the right hire for any role in any type of entrepreneurial business
- A model that will help you strengthen your recruiting intelligence, developing your capacity to hire effectively with the new rules in mind
- The tools to identify candidates who are not only competent but good matches for your entrepreneurship—matches that greatly increase the odds that they'll accept your offer, work with great energy and commitment, and stay for the long term
- A blueprint for success—a way to measure your effectiveness at sourcing, screening, and securing the best candidates for your company

Beyond these benefits, let me tell you what I really hope the book does for you: Hire missionaries to your cause. Because missionaries not only work hard but they work with the passion and commitment that helps entrepreneurs succeed at a higher level. Too often, entrepreneurs make the mistake of hiring people for a role rather than to achieve their mission. The former group is competent. The latter group is competent and driven.

In the increasingly competitive entrepreneurial universe, you need to identify prospective employees who are a cut above "competent." The more people you employ who understand and resonate to your vision, the more likely you can achieve it. This book will put you on the path to this objective.

CHAPTER 1

New Rules
for a
New Age

As you know better than anyone, the entrepreneurial environment has changed dramatically in recent years. It doesn't matter whether you're a sole proprietor working out of your home, a hot tech startup, or an old-fashioned brick-and-mortar business. The world around you is significantly different, and if you don't respond and adapt, you're going to struggle.

Moore's Law, formulated in 1965 by Gordon Moore, the co-founder of Intel, was prescient in its prediction that the number of transistors in an integrated circuit would double about every two years. The larger meaning of the prediction (which has proven to be accurate) is that technological speed increases exponentially. As an entrepreneur, you are well aware of how technology has affected your business. It has brought in new and sometimes unexpected competitors (you're competing with a small company in China that sells to your market via the Internet). It has created all sorts of new selling opportunities for you via social and mobile tools.

While these changes are numerous and varied, they have one overarching effect on entrepreneurs: Hiring the right people in the right way is crucial.

You may be skeptical about how much recruiting has changed, and whether you really need to custom-fit talent to your organization or accept only individuals whose values and work styles are compatible with your company's culture. Perhaps you've experienced a significant amount of success in the past because you came up with a great product or service or hit upon an innovative strategy. I'm not telling you those things aren't important. I'm telling you that they have become less important than people, and that your entrepreneurial mindset may be causing you to doubt this statement.

ASSESS YOUR PERSPECTIVE

How do you define yourself as an entrepreneur? If you're like many people who lead startups or are founders of other types of enterprises, you possess some if not all of the following traits:

- Ambition
- A strong belief in the company, product, or service you created
- Self-confidence
- A near-obsession with financial issues
- Pragmatism
- Trust in instincts

I'm not knocking these traits; they probably helped you build your company. But they also predispose you to focus on individual effort rather than a team approach. They convince you that your ingenuity or the greatness of your product or idea can help the company succeed in the long term. And they cause you to prioritize strategy over recruitment, training, and teamwork.

In his book, *The Hard Thing About Hard Things*, Ben Horowitz, a Silicon Valley entrepreneur turned venture capital investor, talks about how tough it can be to start and run your own business. Horowitz has found that entrepreneurs take on an enormous amount of work as well as an enormous amount of stress. As a result they focus, sometimes myopically, on putting out fires and getting work done through bursts of superhuman effort. Unfortunately, they are so consumed by these tasks that they fail to pay much attention to other ones, such as hiring people who could make it easier for them and help the company become more successful.

Are you this type of entrepreneur? Answering three questions will help you make this assessment. Here's the first one:

Do you think HR is a core process that will make or break the company?

The odds are, you view HR as a secondary function, a way to deal with difficult employees, handle legal matters (i.e., meeting equal opportunity requirements), and fill out forms. You, like many small business owners, see HR as a necessary evil—you know that if you need to involve HR in a business issue, then there's a big problem (like an employee lawsuit). So you have a reflexively negative perspective on human resources.

At the same time, many entrepreneurs are involved in traditional HR process—your HR people may conduct initial employee interviews, for instance, but you're the one who makes the key decisions, especially when it comes to your executive team; and you make those decisions by the seat of your pants. HR, then, does the grunt work, but you or another executive handle the "business" side of human resources.

Here's the second question to determine if you're the traditional entrepreneurial type:

How important do you believe culture is to the company's success?

I don't mean culture as in having an employee game room with ping pong tables and arcade games or putting signs on the wall like "We're All in This Together." These are superficial aspects of culture. Culture is really about values and the types of behaviors that are consistent with these values.

In fact, recruiting for values fit can do more than help your company grow; it may very well allow it to survive disaster. Consider the case of TriNet, a world leader in cloud-based provision of HR services such as payroll, benefits, and employer compliance. TriNet was founded in 1988. By 2000 it had grown to a company of more than 350 employees and was about to go public. Then the dot.com bubble burst. Not only did TriNet founder Martin Babinec have to shelve the IPO post road show, but as revenue plummeted, he had to reduce staff by more than half. The key to surviving what Babinec calls the company's "nuclear winter"? Being able to retain TriNet's best, most highly skilled talent in every division. Even in tough times, these folks were extremely marketable and could have chosen to jump ship. But they believed in TriNet's values and its mission, and they stayed—allowing the company to survive and rebuild as the company rebounded, leading to a successful New York Stock Exchange initial public offering in 2014 and continued growth as a public company today.

Nonetheless, many entrepreneurs don't esteem culture as highly as they do product development, strategy, customer service, finance, and other functions. It's not that they discount culture; even entrepreneurs in the past sought to create a "family atmosphere" in their companies. But they see culture as a luxury, and the other aforementioned functions as necessities. For these entrepreneurs, culture is all about having a good working environment. But they see it as important for morale, not for business results.

And here's the third question:

When push comes to shove, do you feel that you alone are responsible for the company's success?

Entrepreneurs need their egos. You must possess *chutzpah* to be an entrepreneur, to take the risks necessary to succeed. For this reason, it's not unusual for some company founders to believe that they and they alone can save the company when it's in trouble or grow the company when opportunities present themselves. Yes, they value their employees, but they know the business better than anyone and they alone possess the experience and expertise necessary to make the tough decisions and to evaluate what risks are worth taking.

If you answered yes to any or all of the questions, welcome to the club. This entrepreneurial mindset is pervasive and served companies well for years. Today, however, things have changed. Let's look at these three factors and how a new mindset is necessary to succeed in a changing world.

CULTURE EATS
STRATEGY FOR LUNCH

This subhead is a great bumper sticker that all entrepreneurs should stick on their cars. As company after company is discovering, culture isn't a "soft" asset but one that translates directly into productivity and profits. If you are skeptical, think about the world's best companies: Apple, General Electric, Johnson & Johnson. All of them have strong cultures, and all of them recruit and promote people whose values and behaviors align with their cultures.

In entrepreneurial businesses, culture has become equally critical for success. If you look at startups, you'll find that the most successful are the ones that have strong cultures. Salesforce, Facebook, Google, Amazon and others have well-defined cultures and recruit people whose beliefs and behaviors are aligned with these cultures. They do this not because they want to work with people who think and act alike (in fact, they value diversity of ideas and personalities) but because they know that values-consistent cultures create highly profitable companies.

Why is that? Think about a fictional company called Klingon, Inc. If you've ever watched *Star Trek*, you know that Klingons are a highly aggressive race of warriors. So Klingon, Inc. may have the opportunity to hire as their CMO one of the most skilled marketing people on the planet (or planets) who during interviews suggests a marketing strategy that strikes the Klingon leaders as brilliant. But this "ideal" candidate who meets all the specs happens to be a nice guy—he's very laid back, believes in participative decision making and reaching consensus before taking action. If he's hired, he will be a disaster for Klingon, Inc. because his values are antithetical to those of the culture and the Klingon CEO. He will create all sorts of dissension if he's hired, and his poor fit with the culture will subvert whatever marketing contributions he might make.

In the past, companies could live with cultural misfits; entrepreneurial organizations often did. You probably are aware of family businesses where internecine struggles between family members created all sorts of problems—decisions reversed, favorites played, nepotism entrenched. Yet back then, there was a greater margin for "error." Competition wasn't as fierce, and companies with good capital resources and strong products and ideas could overcome an inconsistent cultural composition.

Today, as I outlined in the introduction, financing is plentiful for many reasons—venture capital, low interest rates and so on. Great products and ideas are also abundant, due in large part because of the speed of information and how innovations can be identified and reproduced faster than ever before.

So entrepreneurs need a competitive advantage, and that advantage is a group of people rather than a strong individual at the top. I'm not discounting the value of a strong leader; I'm just suggesting that it's no longer enough.

The most successful startups are often the ones with great, value-consistent teams. Many times, founders create these teams organically; they recruit college friends or other colleagues with whom they share similar visions and work styles. Though they're not consciously trying to create a startup where people share the same mission and values, they do so based on their "natural" recruitment methods. As a result, these startups move forward with astonishing speed and success. They don't get bogged down in counterproductive clashes over how to get things done or in arguments for different agendas. They may (and probably do) have different personalities, skills, and ideas, but they are working in alignment and adding magnitude to their vector because they are all of one mind.

Napoleon Hill, author of *Think and Grow Rich* and other books, talks about how when two brains come together, this melding of minds creates energy; it is the concept behind Mastermind groups, teams of people who rely on "collective intelligence." Michael Leavitt, former Utah governor and former head of the Environmental Protection Agency and Health and Human Services, co-author of *Finding Allies, Building Alliances,* wrote about the need for collaborative effort in the twenty-first century; how the world has become more global, more interconnected and more competitive, favoring agile groups of people with "collaborative intelligence" over the old pyramid and command-and-control structures.

What all this boils down to is that entrepreneurs who recruit the right people will succeed while those who recruit the wrong ones— or who try to do everything themselves—will fail. No less an entrepreneurial guru than Dan Sullivan espouses recruiting as a critical entrepreneurial skill, and he cites a historical example to make this point. Sullivan, founder of Strategic Coach and someone who has provided insightful advice to small business owners for years, views Thomas Edison as the prototype of the modern entrepreneur. When I talked to Dan, he explained, "[Edison] set the model for an individual who is self-made, who comes up with an idea, knows how to organize himself, knows how to put teams [together], knows how to attract investment, knows how to package it, knows how get it out to the marketplace." Right in the middle of reciting this list, Sullivan said that Edison knew how to attract talent and assemble teams, and that's one of the things that made him a giant.

Too often, though, we neglect developing and using this skill, as the following example illustrates.

GROWING LIKE CRAZY,
INSANE RECRUITING

Kevin was the founder and CEO of a New York City–based online marketplace that was one of the fast-growing small companies in the city. Kevin was a great strategist and his previous two startups had also done well, but this one was really taking off, and he needed to add people quickly to keep up with the rapidly expanding business. Kevin, a disruptive innovator, had a grand vision of what his company could be, and he knew that time was of the essence if he wanted to realize it.

The most critical hire he needed to make was for COO. To build the company's infrastructure, people, and processes for scalable growth and to ensure they hit the metrics necessary for the next round of venture funding, Kevin needed to find a COO who was experienced and skilled at these tasks. To find this individual, Kevin contacted a large search firm. Kevin had a connection with one of the firm's partners, and he told him it was critical that they conduct the search as fast as possible to find the individual his company required. The firm partner assured him that they were capable of moving quickly, and within a week they presented a group of candidates to Kevin.

What Kevin didn't know was that the senior partner had assigned the search to a junior partner who was overworked; and that the junior partner was engaged in Level 2 recruiting, which as you'll recall, involves candidates who are available and convenient. In this case, they were people who were "leftovers" from other searches the firm had conducted.

Still, the list of people they presented to Kevin seemed qualified for the position: They had the experience and skills to meet all the job specs. After interviewing the three most promising candidates,

Kevin hired Phil, who seemed to have a bit more experience than the others.

Phil lasted three months. Part of the problem was that he was methodical and cautious, and Kevin was driven by a desire to get things done immediately. Another part of the problem was that Phil didn't share Kevin's vision for the company (even though he indicated in the interview that he did). Phil thought Kevin was a dreamer, that he would bankrupt the company if he moved forward as quickly as he planned; Phil assumed that Kevin would come back down to earth when Phil presented him with a cost study he was making of Kevin's expansion plan. And Phil was a reserved, quiet guy who didn't tell Kevin everything he needed to hear; Phil's communication style drove Kevin nuts. And so they parted ways after three months, requiring Kevin to launch another search for a COO and invest even more time in a task that Kevin wanted completed yesterday.

THE AGE OF ABUNDANCE

You don't have to be a Type A personality like Kevin to want things to be done yesterday. Entrepreneurs live in a world where there is intense pressure for performance. Startups have venture capital people or angel investors wanting a return on their investments—and wanting that return sooner rather than later. Every small business is operating with tighter deadlines than in the past. Even a "sleepy" family business has new competitors; the market leader in their industry who ignored them for years and allowed them to occupy their niche now is eyeing their market and wanting a piece of it.

Even when deadlines aren't imminent and scary, it feels as if they're looming. Data creates a psychological fear of the ticking clock. Every day, we receive information on our devices about competitors, about mergers and acquisitions, about the economy, about new government regulations. All this creates a sense of urgency—we need to act now before it's too late.

This mindset affects entrepreneurial decision making in many areas, but especially when it comes to hiring. Many entrepreneurs are in a rush to fill a position. Whether it's a waiter, an administrative assistant, an accountant, or an executive, they are more interested in speed than accuracy. They prefer to have someone competent in the short term than wait and find an employee who will pay dividends for many years.

As you read this, you may be thinking: "Dave doesn't understand. Every day I don't have someone competent in this job, I'm losing money. It would be great to have someone who would be a productive employee for the next ten years, but I have to be practical."

But being practical today means adopting an abundance mentality rather than one of scarcity. When entrepreneurs stop thinking as they did years ago—that they were one mistake away from bankruptcy—and recognize that numerous options and opportunities exist, then they can free themselves from this belief that beggars can't be choosers and they must make the first decent hire they can.

Author, speaker, and entrepreneur Peter Diamandis writes about this world of abundance, and he makes a convincing case that things are getting better, not worse. He cites many statistics demonstrating that people are more educated, are living longer, and are less violent than years ago. But he also makes the case that the news media creates the perception that things are getting worse: He calls CNN the Crisis News Network because of their focus on death and destruction around the world.

Many entrepreneurs share this negative perception, and it convinces them that:

1. There aren't many good people who can do this job.
2. I should hire the first one who seems capable of doing it.
3. If I wait, I might not find anyone or I might have to hire someone who isn't very good.

This is akin to the twenty-five-year-old guy who decides to marry the first person who shows any interest in him because he's convinced there aren't many good marriage candidates out there and if he waits much longer all the good ones will be taken and he'll go through life as a bachelor.

Yes, the clock is ticking, time is money, and all that. But I would argue that we live in an age of abundance—especially people abundance. Consider that we have this incredible incubator system for entrepreneurs that we never had in the past. The proliferation of startups has produced the perfect training ground for all types of functions and positions. Startups prepare people to take risks, to be agile in their thinking, to innovate. These are skills critical to any entrepreneurial enterprise, and people are acquiring them in startups all over the United States as well as in other countries.

Second, we're seeing more business schools providing formal education for entrepreneurs. Northwestern University, for instance, has the Farley Center for Entrepreneurship and Education, a highly regarded entrepreneurial training program. Other universities also have launched entrepreneurial divisions of their business schools or at least offer courses in entrepreneurship. In fact, if you go to https://www.princetonreview.com/college-rankings?rankings=top-25-entrepreneurship-ugrad, you'll find a list of the top entrepreneurial business schools as ranked by the *Princeton Review* testing service, including a wide range of universities with an even wider range of entrepreneurial offerings.

Third, the best and the brightest no longer want to work at Fortune 500 companies. Many of the people graduating from the top business schools are seeking jobs at startups or hope to join other non-technological small businesses (or start their own). Similarly, a significant percentage of employees are leaving big corporations hoping to land at smaller enterprises that offer greater opportunities to be creative and to have more flexible work environments.

Obviously, it's more difficult to fill some roles than others—if you are looking to fill a leadership position in a company with a distinct culture and you require an unusual mix of skills, then you'll have a smaller pool of candidates than for other positions. Even then, though, you can find the right people if you look the right way. But before addressing what the right way is, we need to understand the concept of alignment and how it helps take companies to the next level.

OPERATING ON
THE SAME WAVELENGTH

When I talk about alignment, I'm not suggesting that entrepreneurs hire people who all think and act alike; that would be a disaster. You need different personalities from different backgrounds to create a diversity of ideas. Creative friction on teams is great. The type of alignment to which I refer involves mission and values.

Consider how quickly entrepreneurial organizations grow today relative to how they used to grow. How long did it take IBM to move from inception to a billion dollar business? The correct answer is sixty-eight years. Relatively recently, it took Facebook nine years to become a billion dollar company. Even more recently,

Instagram hit the billion dollar mark after only nineteen months of existence.

It is not possible to grow this quickly without everyone being on the same page in terms of where the company is heading and the cultural behaviors that are acceptable and unacceptable. There's no time to deal with serious value conflicts. If some people are acting in ways that others feel are unethical, the divide can easily destroy the company—or at the very least create the types of dissension and morale issues that stop them in their tracks.

When people are in alignment, on the other hand, meetings are short, consensus is usually achieved after some discussion and debate, and people are all working toward the same longer-term goal in ways that are consistent with the company culture. In these companies, people don't waste time playing politics or pursuing their own agendas. Instead, they can bypass a lot of the red tape and act with amazing speed and agility. They don't have to waste time with committee meetings and approvals and filling out lots of forms. When they operate with a sense of shared mission and values, they know exactly what they have to do and how to do it.

To achieve alignment, entrepreneurs should focus on recruiting people who possess TSNL potential—they can Take Stuff to the Next Level. This means they're not just getting work done, but they're getting it done in ways that synch with the company's culture and mission. It means they are accomplishing goals in ways that are consistent with what the company believes in. For instance, they aren't just doing a transaction with a supplier but creating a long-term relationship that will benefit both parties. Or they aren't just telling their team members what to do but helping them learn and grow in the process.

TSNLers are capable of getting things done horizontally and vertically. They don't just do stuff; they do stuff in ways that amplify the company culture and pave the way for quantum leaps.

This is the plus of hiring the right people. Just as important, though, is that the more right people you have, the more wrong people you avoid. Think about your current workplace or companies for whom you've worked in the past. Invariably, there are employees who are good at their jobs—they have all the skills their position requires—but who alienate their colleagues for any number of reasons: They humiliate their subordinates, they are loners who can't communicate well, their ethics are questionable, they are arrogant, and so on. Needless to say, they don't function effectively on teams. While they may be able to accomplish necessary tasks in the short run, they do little to foster the values or further the mission of the company.

REASONS FOR
FINDING THE PEOPLE WHO FIT

Here and in the Introductory chapter, I've suggested a number of factors that make hiring the right employees a priority today, including the need for people who can perform well on teams, who can achieve the company's mission rather than just do the job, and who can provide a next-level edge in an increasingly competitive marketplace. But I'd like to expand on these factors or at least translate them into language that will resonate with all different types of entrepreneurs.

To that end, there are three reasons that you require a process to recruit people who fit your company (rather than hire people who only meet the job specs):

The Decreasing Margin for Major Errors

It doesn't matter what type of business you have—hot dog stand or hot tech company—you know that significant mistakes today have much more serious consequences than years ago. That's because mistakes are magnified by technology. For instance, you hire someone who sexually harasses another employee. The harassed employee files a lawsuit, and social media spreads word about the lawsuit. You're in danger of losing customers who hear of the suit and want to know what kind of company you're running that permits this type of behavior. Or perhaps the mistake involves a product recall—one of your developers dropped the ball and failed to perform enough tests to get all the bugs out before the product release. Again, social media spreads the word about this recall with astonishing speed and your stakeholders are upset; you're in danger of losing a major source of funding.

In entrepreneurial companies years ago, a greater tolerance for these types of mistakes existed. Back then, you might have been able to assuage the offended employee and prevented a lawsuit or recalled and reconfigured the flawed product without the whole world knowing about it. You had more time to fix mistakes and you had less competition to take away your disappointed customers.

If you hire the right people, they increase the odds that you won't make these types of mistakes. They may take risks and fail, but they understand the parameters—what is acceptable failure within your culture and given your mission and what is unacceptable.

The Growth Imperative

In the past, entrepreneurs could make a nice life for themselves and for their families by creating a small business and adopting an informal "maintenance" strategy: The company delivered a nice little profit year after year but the founder usually took few risks and was content to maintain the status quo. This strategy is increasingly difficult to sustain in a time of increased competition, higher costs, and rapid rates of change.

Most startups adopt a de facto growth strategy from their inception, and other entrepreneurs are doing likewise. Most entrepreneurs no longer dream of increasing profits incrementally from one year to the next. Instead, they dream of franchising their initial concept; or moving from local to global; or of identifying and tapping into emerging markets; or transitioning from a brick-and-mortar business to a digital one. To chug along with marginal profits year after year or to try and maintain the same product mix, marketing, and so on annually is a much tougher challenge today than years ago. Entrepreneurs need and want to grow, and you can't grow organically without people who fit your company.

Remember our discussion of alignment. You need people who are aligned with your mission if you want to become a bigger and better company. They are the ones who won't just meet deadlines and accomplish tasks but will do so with a larger purpose in mind. They will help grow their own direct reports so they can add more value in the long term. They will forge relationships with suppliers, customers, and other stakeholders that will lead to better opportunities.

You need people who are not only thinking about the task at hand but who are thinking ahead. They're the ones who will help you evolve rather than just maintain what you have.

The Need for Speed

Two heads are better—and faster—than one. Entrepreneurs are often one-person gangs. If you're the founder of a small company, how many times have you been frustrated by how slowly your people seem to be working and said or thought, "I can do this faster myself." Individual effort has always been a signature of entrepreneurial companies. Rugged individualism—whether on the part of the CEO or her people—has been the type of behavior encouraged historically. The employee who works over the weekend or through the night to finish a project is a small business hero.

But if speed is the goal—and it often is in a volatile, ultra-competitive marketplace—then businesses need people who can work well together. Teams of employees who are attuned to their company's culture and long-term goals can operate with remarkable speed. They don't have to keep knocking on the boss's door and asking permission for this and that. They recognize what "growth hacks" are acceptable with their culture. They are willing to sacrifice their egos for the greater good—this means that they don't slow up progress because they're pursuing their own agendas. Perhaps most important of all, their alignment helps avoid the sort of conflict that turns one-hour meetings into endless debates. They all recognize the end goal and how to achieve it, and so they don't get bogged down in the types of personal feuds and obstructionist tactics that prevent quick decisions and action.

Once you're convinced of the value of fit, you need to think about the next recruiting issue that is very much a product of our current environment: the challenge of prying the right person out of a current—and often very good—job.

CHAPTER 2

Slow Down, Use a Process, Move Beyond the Specs

The title of this chapter will strike many of you as heretical. Entrepreneurs may be wildly different in terms of their businesses, personalities, and strategies, but most of them like to move quickly, fly by the seat of their pants, and lust after expertise.

But if you apply these traits to recruiting, you will come up short because:

- It takes time to find the candidate whose beliefs and personal missions are consistent with those of the company
- Instinct may help you find people you like but not necessarily people who will deliver maximum value to the company
- Expertise only guarantees that candidates possess the skill to do the job, not that they will do it well or for long

In the last chapter, I detailed how the entrepreneurial environment has changed and why a shift in recruiting consciousness is necessary. Here, I'll suggest some specific actions you can take to facilitate this shift. First, though, I want to give you an example of how this shift can pay off in a big way—how it can help snag a candidate that you might never have had a chance of securing in the past.

THE TORTOISE WON THIS RACE

A paradox is at work in today's entrepreneurial enterprise. In the previous chapter, I discussed how a need for speed is crucial in a highly competitive environment, and how hiring employees with a shared sense of mission and values helps get things done faster. At the same time, moving slower in the recruiting process is equally important, since it takes time to find candidates who possess a shared mission and values.

Movable Ink was the next generation of email marketing companies, and their ability to tailor a message to a given target market faster and more effectively than other companies had made it one of the world's hottest startups. I was brought in to help the company find a VP of talent.

Many of the Movable Ink candidates met the specs: They possessed exactly the right talent acquisition and industry experience necessary for the role, and they were strong leaders who grew and motivated their people. I identified a handful of candidates who were the best of the best, but all of them were doing well in top positions with great companies. Why would they want to leave?

I discussed the issue with Vivek Sharma, Movable Ink's founder.

"It's highly unlikely we can pry away any of these candidates by offering them money or perks or trying to convince them that Movable Ink is the best company on the face of the earth."

"Then what can we do?"

"We can see if one of them views the world as you do."

This may sound like a simple task, but in reality, it requires time and a structured process to discern a candidate who has compatible beliefs and goals. It's not like you can interview a candidate and get a sense that she is the one. When you are searching for an intangible such as values, you need to take your time and create a plan to make this challenging determination.

Part of the time involves an entrepreneur exploring and articulating what his values are. When I asked Vivek to do this, he was perplexed for a moment. But by relying on a tried-and-true process, I was able to elicit the necessary information. We began talking about Movable Ink and the vision Vivek had for the company, how he believed in curiosity tethered to empathy and grit as the sources of innovation and the qualities his most successful team members valued.

Then, we began to assess the values of the candidates, again using a process that helped us identify mismatches as well as matches. We began to see how some of the candidates would never succeed or last at Movable Ink—one had a fixed mindset, another was too self-centered, a third was too closed off to her colleagues.

One candidate, however, was different. It wasn't that she was more brilliant or more accomplished as a talent leader than the other candidates. It was simply that Louise Peddell's beliefs and values mirrored Vivek's. As we analyzed the values match, we saw that they both were servant leaders: curious, determined, and focused on their companies' greater good. Though they weren't clones from a personality standpoint, their values were aligned.

Vivek recognized this values fit, and wanted Louise for the job.

We also conveyed to Louise how she and Vivek had this extraordinary simpatico vision and how this was a once-in-a-lifetime match: She resonated with what Vivek and Movable Ink were all about. This recognition prompted her to leave a terrific job that almost anyone else would wish for and join Movable Ink.

Yes, this recruiting effort took a bit more time and effort than other searches. And yes, the decision wasn't made by an assessment of a candidate's expertise and experience (though Louise had plenty of both) as much as by identifying the candidate who would thrive in Movable Ink's culture and resonate to Vivek's style of leadership. And yes, I'm sure going about the recruiting process this way may have made Vivek a little uncomfortable initially.

Vivek chose this slower, structured, values-focused process again when we partnered to secure other key leaders, including his Chief Marketing Officer, SVP Sales, Chief Financial Officer, VP Product and an independent board member.

LEADERSHIP JOB #1: RECRUITING

I cannot state this principle enough: Recruitment is too critical a responsibility for leaders to delegate. So like Vivek, you have to make a commitment to recruiting the right way. I know, you're incredibly busy and have too much on your plate. But as the founder and head of the company, you're in the best position to assess whether a given individual possesses your values and fits your vision of what the company can become. Many entrepreneurs lack the time or impulse to communicate their vision or values. They keep it locked in their heads, so their HR people or whoever is doing the hiring isn't aware of the entrepreneur's vision of what the company might be or the types of people who might help achieve this vision.

Now, this doesn't mean that you have to get involved with the nitty-gritty of the hiring process. Your HR people as well as an outside firm can handle many of the tasks. But you do need to be involved and play a key role, especially when the hire is someone who can have a significant impact on the company. You have to ensure a structured process is understood by all and implemented consistently. And you have to make sure a values assessment is part of the process.

Here is a sampling of the type of questions this process should answer:

> If a candidate appears overly sensitive, does it seem like he will struggle in a straight talk culture?

> Does a candidate for a managerial position have the capacity to mentor others and grow the company the way you want it grown?

> Will someone who is a great individual contributor possess the agility to work well on teams; is her expertise matched by her willingness to collaborate?

While leaders can help answer these questions if they're involved in hiring, they can't do so if they fail to subscribe to the following principles:

- Recruiting has become a leadership competency and leaders must strive to improve their abilities in this area.
- These abilities require not only learning how to interview and assess candidates in terms of values but recognizing when a values match has been made.

Putting these principles into practice requires a recruiting consciousness. It's no longer just a task but integral to the company's sustainability. The leaders who recruit best become almost evangelical in their desire to bring in the right people for their companies. They see their companies as reflections of themselves, and they attempt to bring in the best people in order to help their companies become the best versions of themselves.

Leaders must also recruit with great transparency and honesty. Jack Welch has said that truth, trust, and transparency are critical leadership tenets. This is as opposed to titles, false appearances, and covering up mistakes. Leaders who recruit superbly are people who are honest and open with candidates about what their companies represent, and in turn, they practice what they preach. They communicate what they value and make sure that the company's practices reflect these values. In this way, they create alignment. They avoid the cognitive dissonance that exists in many organizations— where leaders say one thing but actually value other things. (For instance: Saying we are all about creating win-win situations with our partners but shortchanging vendors routinely.)

This dissonance will sabotage the recruiting process. Not only will good people leave when they realize a leader has deceived them, but in this age of transparency, social media and other digital sources will communicate quickly what the company's real values are (as opposed to what a leader says they are).

Perhaps more than anything else, leaders who recruit well are proactive in the process. They dig in early to find candidates and dig in deeper over time to find the right ones. They don't sift through resumes searching for nuggets. They are well aware of a conclusion drawn by Lazlo Bock in his book, *Work Rules*. Bock, Google's head of People Operations, believes that resumes as a recruiting tool are a thing of the past. Instead, Google is much more interested in other approaches to determine if a given candidate is a good fit for their company.

One of their recruiting strategies is to target what they refer to as passive job-seekers—individuals who already have excellent jobs and aren't looking to change companies. Google knows, however, that some of the best potential hires aren't actively seeking to be hired by Google, but if they were, they'd be ideal matches. As a result, Google identifies these potential hires, keeps track of them, and when they are ready to make a move, Google is ready for them.

It's fascinating that Google, a company that spends a significant amount of money on recruiting, spends relatively little on training. That's because once they make a good match—once they find a candidate whose beliefs and work style align with Google's culture—these candidates adapt and learn quickly on their own.

Most of you don't run entrepreneurial businesses anywhere close to the size of Google—at least yet. But if you aspire to grow your business, you should take a cue from Google and target happily employed people. Have lunch with them. Find out more about them. If they seem like a good match, let them know you're interested when they become interested. Because of high job liquidity, some of them are likely to be looking for a job sooner rather than later, even though they may not know it yet.

Go beyond this and become a talent facilitator. Get out there and make introductions, even if there is no direct benefit for you. If a fellow entrepreneur contacts you looking to hire someone, make suggestions of who they might consider. Bring a diverse group of people in your field together for lunches, coffee, workshops. Attend conferences and breakout sessions where you're likely to meet new people. Participate in social media forums. All this will accomplish two goals: help you broaden your talent circle and create reciprocity (you help others find people they need and they in turn will help you).

I've done these things my entire career, and it has given me access to a broader range of talent and encouraged others to assist me when I'm searching for a particular executive. Mary Lou Song was one of eBay's first five employees hired, and helped build a $40 billion business. She is widely credited with creating the public relations, community, and product strategies that helped grow their membership into the millions. When she was at eBay, the company went through such massive growth that it catalyzed her own professional growth. I first met Mary Lou in New York City when she was leading the product team at a Gerson Lehrman Group company. Some time later, I remembered how impressed I had been by Mary Lou's values-driven approach, how she hungered to take on challenges and make a difference, and how growth and contribution resonated so strongly with a couple of entrepreneur friends who were also in San Francisco. I introduced her to two entrepreneur friends, Rick Teed and Butch Haze, precisely because they too shared these values. Together, they've created a new direct response video company that promises to disrupt the entire advertising technology industry.

YOU DON'T NEED STARS
FOR THE COMPANY TO SHINE

Or rather, you don't have to recruit stars to create tremendous growth and profitability. The mistake many entrepreneurs make is thinking that to take the company to the next level, they need to go out there and find the best marketer, money guy, software designer, and engineer for the next ten years. They possess the George Steinbrenner/New York Yankee mentality: Buy lots of superstar free agents.

Better, instead, to follow the lead of Theo Epstein, formerly of the Boston Red Sox and now of the Chicago Cubs: Develop talent to fit the culture you build. If you recruit people who possess the basic competencies required to do the job and who are aligned with your vision and values, you can grow them and they will in turn grow the business. You can always train and develop them to become better leaders and managers, programmers, and salespeople. If they are in synch with your culture—if their beliefs about work and goals for their careers are well-suited to your company—then they will do everything they can to improve their skills and reach stretch goals. They may not be superstars when they arrive at your doorstep, but they will become super-performers precisely because your company feels like home to them. As my mentor Keith Cunningham says, "You only have to get the anchor one inch off the bottom of the ocean floor for the ship to move forward."

In an April 6, 2015 *Harvard Business Review* article, Daniel Freedman wrote about the myth of recruiting stars. Based on a number of studies, Freedman concluded that recruiting top talent and paying them accordingly wasn't worth it; that people who delivered outstanding results at one company often couldn't replicate that performance at their next employer; and that outstanding performance usually happened when an individual's work preferences and requirements were well-suited to the employer.

This doesn't mean you should ignore talent. It does mean that for that talent to blossom, a match must be made between the individual's preferences and values and those of the company.

The good news, then, is that even if you're a cash-strapped startup who can't afford to pay superstar salaries, you can still recruit an outstanding performer who will accept reasonable compensation. But you have to be thoughtful, strategic, and structured as you go about the process of finding this individual. I'll provide you with more specific steps to achieve this goal in chapters 5 through 8, but keep the following overarching principles in mind:

Think Through Your Mission and Strategic Priorities

The great Greek Stoic Epictetus said "First say to yourself what you would be; and then do what you have to do." Too often, leaders fail to clarify in their own minds what their business represents. Entrepreneurs are often so focused on the daily challenges—on satisfying an unsatisfied customer, on fixing problematic software—that they don't reflect on their long-term goal and how they intend to achieve it. This reflection, though, yields a great recruiting pitch. What you're selling job candidates is an opportunity to learn, to grow, to be part of something that reflects who they are and who they want to be. When you know what your company represents and where it's going, you can offer candidates the opportunity to join an enterprise that seems tailor-made for them. This can entice even the best people out of great jobs, since you're offering them a chance to become a better version of themselves. If you doubt this statement, consider that we've recruited top engineering candidates from companies like Google, Facebook, and Uber who often receive four additional job offers within a six-week span. This translates to 500 percent negative unemployment. Yet they leave their jobs if the new offer resonates with them on a deeper level.

Romance the Offer

I'm not suggesting you should paint a false picture of your company or its prospects. Recognize, though, that to paraphrase the Army's ad slogan, you're not just selling a job, you're selling an adventure. When Sir Ernest Shackleton was recruiting sailors for his Antarctic expedition, he created the following ad:

Men Wanted: For hazardous journey. Small wages, bitter cold,
long months of complete darkness, constant danger, safe return
doubtful. Honour and recognition in case of success.

Despite the forbidding tone and content of his ad, Shackleton found plenty of recruits. That's because his "hook" was honor and recognition and the unstated prospect of great adventure. For some men, this was their raison d'être. They were willing to give up the comfort of warm homes and safe jobs for the chance to fulfill a larger purpose.

But as leader-recruiters, you need to convey this purpose clearly and with motivation. By describing the values the company espouses and the vision you have for it in compelling terms, you allow job candidates to envision whether this is a place they want to be. If it is, they will be willing to go on an adventure with you, even if you're not offering the highest salary or the greatest working conditions.

Keep Reminding Yourself That Technical Chops Are Only 20 Percent of the Solution

This is the most challenging principle to which you must adhere and so I'm going to keep reminding you to remind yourself throughout the book. If you're running a restaurant, you want to hire the chef who can cook the best. If you're in charge of a sales-driven organization, you are trying to hire salespeople who are great at convincing customers to buy. If you're a tech startup, you want brilliant software designers.

Competence is important, and you may make some hires primarily for a given individual's expertise. But for jobs of significance—especially managerial and leadership roles—focus on an individual's values and fit with the culture. You can train people so they increase their level of expertise, but you can't train them to have the values you require. Therefore, when you look at all the candidates out there, be flexible about knowledge and skills and inflexible when it comes to values.

AVOID MASKS BUT ACCEPT BLIND SPOTS

Let's say you have interviewed a number of candidates for a top position with your company, and you've winnowed the list down to two people, both of whom have roughly equal amounts of expertise and experience. You know both of them can handle the job from a task standpoint, but each of the candidates has a distinct personality. Tom is highly confident and not shy about describing his past achievements. At times, he can even be somewhat arrogant, but you understand that he has a lot to be arrogant about.

Alice, on the other hand, is much more restrained when talking about herself. Though she's quietly confident, she has to be pushed to relate her successes. During the interview, Alice deflects compliments and points to the contributions of others that helped her company achieve objectives; she talks a lot about the importance of her team.

Tom is clearly a take-charge, decisive manager who is good at telling people what to do and getting things done quickly. Alice's managerial style is less decisive but more reliant on creating synergies among her people; she works more slowly and is more interested in soliciting input from others before making a decision.

Who would you hire? In the old work paradigm, most people would choose Tom. In a command-and-control hierarchy, Tom's approach works best. As a factory foreman, a COO, or an IT executive, Tom would demand respect and accountability and get things done efficiently.

In the new work paradigm, Alice is a better choice. Obviously, your hiring decisions depend on many factors, and it may be that an assertive, decisive candidate is a better choice for your company than a more egalitarian, less assertive one. My point is simply that in today's world, entrepreneurs need staff who are able to work well with others, who can sacrifice their personal agendas for group goals, and who want their organizations to grow and achieve greatness.

So much of entrepreneurial success these days is dependent on collaboration. It's also dependent on managerial agility. In a liquid workplace, managers must be able to work with an ever-changing cast of characters; they must be able to get new people up to speed quickly, to integrate them seamlessly into teams. People with huge egos often lack this agility as well as the collaborative impulse.

As a general rule, humility is a much better trait to seek in employees than hubris. Of course, people can fake humility and hide hubris, so it's not always easy to differentiate candidates based on these two factors. A better differentiator involves masks versus blind spots. People who wear masks are trying consciously to hide something from others . . . or themselves. They lack the ability to be vulnerable because this would make it possible for others to see who they really are—and for various reasons, they don't want others to see their true personae. These people are likely to be drama llamas, creating all sorts of workplace stress as the tension between who they really are and how they present themselves roils within. People who have blind spots, on the other hand, don't realize what they are hiding from themselves (i.e., that they don't like confrontation) but are capable of being open, vulnerable, and compassionate. They are innocently ignorant, and if they are sufficiently humble, they come to be aware of their growth opportunities, and with this awareness, they start addressing this hidden potential, learning and improving their capabilities while expanding their capacity.

Here is a list of Mask versus Blind Spot traits to help you identify both types:

MASK

- ► Hiding something, protecting ego
- ► Pretends to know it all, have all the answers
- ► Causes of failure are all external faults, others to blame
- ► Strategy was wrong
- ► Things outside of their control are to blame
- ► Victims of circumstance
- ► Job hopping
- ► Strong motivation to work driven by survival, need for money, scarcity mindset
- ► Entitled self-interest
- ► Uses hubris and pomposity to hide lack of self-confidence

BLIND SPOTS

- ► Innocent deficit of knowledge, data, or insight
- ► Prefer working with good people to the prestige of working for a hot company
- ► Not afraid to be vulnerable
- ► Self-admit gaps of knowledge
- ► Open, perhaps even eager to learn
- ► Strong emotional need to work driven by becoming something more, achieving great things, making life better for others
- ► Compassionate interest in others
- ► Humility
- ► Guided by truth, wisdom, and not afraid to admit lack of experience

Targeting this latter group of traits can give you a recruiting competitive edge. Other companies are still focused on people with technical chops and don't mind that they've moved from job to job, that they're arrogant, and that they exhibit a scarcity mindset. If you can focus on finding people who are honest about their shortcomings, who display empathy, and who are avid learners, you will find that you have a lot of potentially great job candidates from which to choose.

Be assured that there are plenty of people like this available to entrepreneurs. As a society, we are still obsessed with the best and the brightest. Malcolm Gladwell, in his now-famous article in *The New Yorker* titled "The Talent Myth," made a convincing case that the McKinsey Consulting Group and Enron had overvalued "smart people"; that just because someone did well at a prestigious school or had a high IQ didn't mean that he would deliver great performance. Gladwell cited companies like Wal-Mart and Procter & Gamble as consistently successful companies that avoided paying through the nose for Ivy League talent, instead creating organizational structure, culture, and strategy that created positive results over the long term.

Most entrepreneurs don't have access to a lot of Harvard MBA job applicants. People who worked for a top consulting firm generally want their next position to be at either hot tech companies like Google or major corporations like Johnson & Johnson. In the past, this may have seemed like a disadvantage. Today, though, the people with the qualities you seek—vulnerability, a love of learning, compassion—are available in an ever-widening pool.

DIG FOR CORE MOTIVATIONS AND REASONS BEHIND DECISIONS

Given that you're going to be interviewing a lot of promising people, you need to develop an approach that will help you find the individuals who are right for you and your company. This means moving away from the standard operating procedure, in which you ask people to describe their accomplishments and recount how they developed their expertise, while you try to ascertain if they have the skills they claim.

If you're like most entrepreneurs—and if you have been involved in the hiring process—you probably ask candidates questions like:

- What would you say is your most significant achievement?
- Can you give me an example of when you used your knowledge and skills to meet a challenging work goal?
- What would you say is the most important thing you've learned in your career, and how did you apply this learning to help your company?

There's nothing wrong with these questions, but they don't go sufficiently deep to assess candidates' values. Therefore, consider these two tactics during interviews: paying attention to *what motivated people* and *why they made the decisions they did*.

Think of all the possible work motivations an individual might have: a corner office (and other perks), salary, title, prestige (working for a top company), maximizing her talent, helping a company grow and prosper, making a difference, changing the world. Most people have multiple motivations, but you need to ascertain the primary one. Motivations exist on a continuum, with the ones on the left being the "basest" (i.e., having a corner office) and the ones on the right being the most noble (changing the world).

In a liquid job marketplace, people with primarily base motivations are apt to leave your company at the drop of a hat—or a better offer. Therefore, dig deep when discussing what motivated them to take a given action. For instance: "I see that you left Company X when things were going great; why did you decide to leave and join company Y?" Ideally, the answer to this question will be something like, "I thought Company Y was moving in a direction that was better suited to my own goals and work styles." As opposed to: "They offered me a lot more money." Just as important, motivations reveal values. Are you motivated by the opportunity to change a marketplace by bringing out a revolutionary new product? Or are you motivated by all the money you can make by doing so? Obviously, motivation is a more complex issue than these two simple alternatives represent, but by digging down and determining what drives an individual, you can assess how her values fit with your company.

In addition, capitalize on the transparency offered by social media by ascertaining if the motivation cited by a candidate matches up with reality. For instance, someone may have told you how much he believes in working in a culture aligned with his values, but when you check his posts on Facebook, you discover a rant about how his former employer didn't give him a good bonus which is why he left the company. On the other hand, you might also discover that a candidate posted something on LinkedIn that confirms exactly what he told you about why he took a specific action.

The second tactic: Talk to candidates about significant decisions they've made. Why did they decide to go into advertising? Why did they take off a year to work for a charitable cause? Why did they initiate a program at a former employer to facilitate information flow across all functions and levels?

Big decisions offer entrepreneurs insights into what makes people tick. Do you want to hire someone who chose a career because he thought it was a glamorous profession? Or do you think someone will fit better in your company if she chose the profession because she thought it gave her the best opportunity to make her mark and grow as a person and a professional?

I recognize that investigating decisions and motivations may not be top of mind issues for entrepreneurs looking to hire people. Entrepreneurs are often pragmatic—they have an opening, and they want to find the most qualified person. As a result, they direct the selection process so that the focus is on competencies and accomplishments. Who can do the job best today? But consider that you no longer have to limit yourself to this pragmatic mindset. In today's marketplace, people often change jobs every five years (or less). There are also many more candidates than in the past who have gone through training programs or received education that makes them qualified (from a competency standpoint) to do the jobs you need to fill. With this larger pool of qualified candidates to choose from, you don't have to settle for the merely qualified; you can look beyond present capabilities to future contributions. Who is the candidate who will help take the company where you want it to go? Who possesses the values that are congruent with your beliefs? By focusing on decisions and motivations, you can answer these questions in ways that will benefit your company.

MAINTAIN YOUR COMPANY'S VALUES TO KEEP THE RIGHT PEOPLE ON BOARD

Entrepreneurial leaders are their companies' values custodians and amplifiers. This may seem like a minor responsibility compared with profit and loss and introducing new products and services, but here's why it's major: If you allow values to weaken and disappear, all your recruiting efforts will be for naught. All the great people you worked so hard to bring into the company through a slower, structured process will flee.

Here's a cautionary tale that illustrates this point—a tale that I observed firsthand. After we sold HotJobs to Yahoo for $486 million, I was asked to fly out and meet Yahoo's Head of HR in their Sunnyvale headquarters. We had a three and a half hour meeting with twenty-one other people. We sat around the most beautiful conference room table I had ever seen—it was carved from a two hundred-year-old sequoia.

As we sat there and discussed the business, I heard many stories about elaborate parties that people would fly to from around the country as well as about Yahoo's culture of harmony. What I didn't hear about was exciting initiatives, innovative approaches to problems, and effective plans to help the company grow in a changing environment. Once upon a time, Yahoo's culture was one of great industriousness and diligence. They worked with zeal and creativity, and they were especially astute in their acquisition strategy. But over time, the company had become fat and lazy—they were victims of the stock option syndrome. Many executives had become paper millionaires very quickly and at a young age. It was up to the leadership to maintain the original values that had put them on the map, and the leadership let the company down.

A few months after the meeting at the sequoia table, I departed the company, recognizing that my own core values and those of Yahoo would clash—that I would never be able to learn, grow, and thrive in their culture.

Yahoo could have become Google. Instead, it became a shadow of its former self, selling to Verizon for far less than it might have received years earlier. The saddest part of the story is that it didn't have to happen. Yahoo lost a lot of good people besides myself—people who once had resonated to the original values of Yahoo's founders but found themselves working for a company with which they no longer had much in common. The great American writer Will Durant said, "A nation is born stoic, and dies epicurean." This is too often true in business.

The following graphic is one I would urge every leader who wants to maintain core values to put on the office wall:

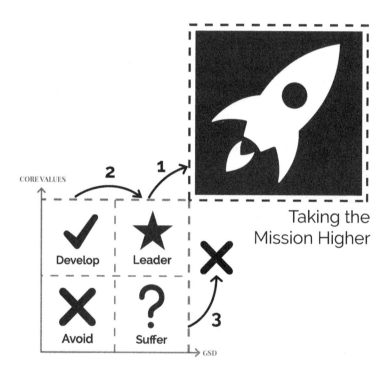

To download this PDF and other resources, go to
www.HireSmartFromTheStart.com

As you can see, the upper two quadrants on the y-axis (or "why" axis) represent people who possess the Core Values that match those of the organization. In the lower two quadrants, people lack these values. In the upper right and lower right quadrants, these individuals are adept and Get Stuff Done (GSD).

The most successful entrepreneurs understand (consciously or not) that if they hire people in the upper two quadrants (who possess the Core Values), they will be bringing in people who will thrive and Take Stuff to the Next Level (TSNL): (1) Even those in the upper left quadrant who may not be great at implementing and generating results at the moment (they lack some technical chops to Get Stuff Done) can be trained to become better at execution; they can be developed into leaders. (2) On the other hand, people who lack the right values can't be trained to be empathetic or to work collaboratively; it's either in you or it's not; they often get blocked from moving up by the defenders of the company's Core Values. (3) As tempting as it may be to recruit individuals in the lower right quadrant—they may tempt you with their high level of skills and track record for generating results—they poison the values well. They will create conflicts both internally (with team members) and externally (with clients/customers, vendors, and others).

Therefore, take your role as values custodian seriously. It requires a bit more work, thought, and structure to fulfill this role, but it's worth it.

CHAPTER 3

Recruiting Myths and Realities

M any entrepreneurs will admit to hiring mistakes, but they aren't always aware of the cause of these mistakes. With hindsight, they recognize that they settled for a second-tier candidate when they might have attracted a top-tier one; or that they hired someone who was qualified for the job but not a good match for the company; or that they assumed that they'd attract a slew of great applicants but instead attracted a lot of mediocre ones.

Even the smartest entrepreneurs make these mistakes because they're easy mistakes to make. If you're not fully invested or lack experience in the recruiting process, then you will probably hire the wrong person.

This lack of experience and investment makes you vulnerable to recruiting myths—myths that have gained traction over the years among all types of entrepreneurs. Two myths in particular cause entrepreneurs to make hiring mistakes:

- **The Myth of Greatness:** Our company is so terrific, our products and services are so amazing, that the best and the brightest will be falling all over themselves to apply for our job openings.

- **The Myth of Smallness:** Our company is relatively insignificant compared to the larger companies or the market leaders; none of the top candidates would want to work here.

As you can see, these two myths are opposites, and entrepreneurs often recruit under the influence of one of them. Let's examine how this is so.

THE MYTHS IN ACTION

Sam graduated from a top business school and spent a few years working for (and doing well at) a large Silicon Valley company before he decided to strike out on his own. Partnering with two fellow business school graduates, they came up with an app that their mentor—a well-known business school professor—told them was one of the best new products he'd seen in years. Sam quickly found angel investors who put a significant amount of money into the company, and the buzz in Silicon Valley was that Sam's company might be the next big thing.

Needing to staff up quickly, Sam put the word out (through his contacts as well as via Internet job sites) that he was hiring, and he assumed that he would be inundated with calls from the best engineering, marketing, and finance people in the Valley. In fact, he received a much smaller than anticipated response, and most of the applicants lacked the skills and experience Sam required. He did receive an application from one individual who did possess these skills and experience, but when Sam pitched her on the benefits of receiving a certain amount of equity in the company (to compensate for the relatively low salary) this candidate quickly said she wasn't interested.

Sam's launch was delayed by almost a year. During that time, Sam had to do another round of fundraising among investors to gain additional funds for salaries. He also had to hire an outside recruiting consultant to do the hard work of searching for, finding, and selling key people on joining the company. As a result of the delay, two other competitors with similar apps entered the marketplace ahead of Sam, and as of this writing, he's still playing catch-up.

With hindsight, it's easy to see that Sam bought into the myth of greatness. In his small pond, he was a big fish. Based on the encouragement of his professor, his partners, and the Silicon Valley grapevine, Sam was convinced that top people would beat a path to his door. Like some other entrepreneurs who experience initial success, he was convinced that much greater success was assured and that others would feel likewise.

Now consider Terri. After college, she worked for a series of retailers in sales and did well, being promoted to regional sales manager for one national chain. Then she took some time off to have children and decided to go back to work when her kids were entering high school. Her goal was to start her own business: She wanted to start a service that provided new moms with support and a variety of services during the first year of their babies' lives. Terri did her research, became certified as a doula, and enlisted a few friends in her project. She combined personal home visits with home-baked meals and a website that only subscribers to her service had access to.

The business started slowly, but after almost two years, Terri had more business than she could handle—mostly from word-of-mouth in her suburban town. A friend of her husband's was a consultant, and when he heard about what Terri was doing, he suggested that she consider expanding the business throughout the metro area. He created a business plan, brought in some investors, and explained to Terri that she needed to hire a few people, especially a marketing manager (promoting the business via digital and traditional media was central to his plan).

Terri placed an ad for a marketing manager, but she was less than impressed with the candidates—most of them either lacked sufficient experience or the type of knowledge she was sure was essential for success. What she really wanted was to hire someone who had helped a small business expand regionally through a savvy marketing strategy. But rather than expand her search, Terri settled for a candidate who she liked and thought would be fun to work with, even though he lacked the drive and savvy that Terri had hoped for.

For Terri, the myth of smallness made her aim too low. She convinced herself that her business was too insignificant to attract the candidates she wanted. Plus, she knew she couldn't pay them the salary that she assumed they'd demand. Rather than test the waters and develop a plan to make a critical hire, she settled for a lesser candidate.

A LIMITED PERSPECTIVE

For Terri, Sam, and millions of other entrepreneurs, these myths have a powerful hold on their thinking. I understand that it's a natural result of their entrepreneurial experiences. But to do a better job of bringing in the right people, they need to broaden their perspective.

Many small business owners like Terri view their ability to attract talent with skepticism. Consider the typical owners of local plumbing businesses. It may be a good business that provides the owner with a nice living, and it probably grew slowly but surely over the years. When the owner had to hire people, he usually leaned on his network of friends and family; his Uncle Joe had a cousin who knew someone who wanted to get in the trades. So the owner naturally draws from this network when he has to hire someone.

But what if this plumbing business had an opportunity to grow in a much more significant way? What if the owner had developed a specialized method of basement waterproofing that was more effective and less expensive than other methods on the market? If she wants to grow and scale this business, it's unlikely that Uncle Joe will have a cousin who can help her. To find the people who not only possess the necessary expertise and experience but who share this plumber's mission and values, the search must expand beyond a limited network. Unfortunately, this plumber may not think in these terms; she may believe that the individual who helped her develop a yellow pages ad will be equal to the task of developing a regional advertising campaign. Or, of even greater concern, she may not even consider how a potential job candidate might contribute to a growing company's culture; how a managerial candidate might grow and develop young people, model ways of working for others, deal with conflict, and so on. These qualities may not be matter when it's a three-person local shop, but if an entrepreneur has a bigger vision, then they're vitally important. If these entrepreneurs are burdened by the Myth of Smallness, they won't think to search beyond the borders of their experience.

Being positive and proactive about your ability to recruit is an antidote to this myth. Irving Grousbeck has taught at Stanford Business School for over thirty years and has probably done more than anyone to bring entrepreneurial studies front and center in the business school world—helping shape countless business leaders

and enterprises in the process. In Grousbeck's estimation, if entrepreneurs find themselves needing to fill key managerial roles and
they lack internal candidates, they haven't been doing a very good
job as leaders.

To avoid this problem, Grousbeck believes in recruiting for "upside
potential"—people who can expand their responsibilities as the company grows. To do so, however, you need to possess the confidence
that high-potential people will want to work for you; that they'll be
willing to join your company not because you're offering them the
best compensation package or the most prestigious company name
but because your goals and values resonate with their own.

At the other end of the confidence spectrum, we find a different type of limited perspective. Some people—especially relatively
young entrepreneurs in hot sectors like technology, food, and fash-
ion—have enjoyed a great deal of early success. They've done well
in school, obtained a terrific first job, were seen as fast-trackers
and then opened a business with lots of financial, mentor, and peer
support.

Their perspective is limited by two factors. First, they are focused
solely on outward signs of achievement—the schools people went to,
the organizations they're members of, the awards they've won, the
successes they've enjoyed. As a result, they only want to hire people
who have achieved in these ways—people who are mirror images
of themselves. Second, they can't imagine that potential job candidates would view their businesses differently than they do. For most
of their adult lives, people have showered them with praise, and so
they are convinced that others will immediately gravitate toward
their vision of their companies.

As a result, they either are turned down by lots of top people or
look for the wrong types of employees. The Myth of Greatness convinced them they need to load up on expertise and they don't need to

be concerned if a candidate fits their culture and mission; and they are blind to how top candidates view them and their companies.

Beware of the three lies entrepreneurs tell themselves:

1. We're the hottest game in town.
2. We hire the best people.
3. We have the best culture.

These lies all feed the Myth of Greatness and create dangerously narrow perspectives. They make you feel like the only hires worth making are creative geniuses and charismatic characters; you're more like a casting director going for a certain look rather than substance. I knew an entrepreneur who told me that he wanted to hire "fun" people. His tech company reflected that desire: He had more video games than many arcades, no set hours for employees, and an open, laid-back culture that encouraged a free exchange of ideas. It was a fun place to work, but it went out of business two years after it made an initial splash in the marketplace.

I'm not against fun, but if it's all play and little work, then a company isn't long for this world. That's especially true if recruitment prioritizes fun qualities—humor, adventurousness, coolness—over industriousness. While successful entrepreneurs may attribute many factors to their success, they all consistently hire industrious people—individuals who work hard, produce a lot, and generate results. Perhaps more to the point, they aren't limited by their own sense of superiority. They get that the work has to get done for the company to achieve its objectives, so they're open to any candidate who looks like he or she can execute.

RECRUITING MISTAKES CAUSED BY MYTHS

Under the influence of a myth, entrepreneurs can make what seem like sound hiring choices but in fact are bringing in underperforming employees at best and saboteurs at worst. I've touched on some of the mistakes earlier, but it's useful to highlight them here so that you have top-of-mind awareness of what they are.

Myth of Smallness Mistakes

- **Underbudgeting for a key position.** The thinking goes, "There's not much point in spending a lot to fill this job, since even if we somehow manage to land the best possible candidate, she'll probably leave as soon as she gets the chance." Many entrepreneurs have cost-containment mindsets, and while you certainly need to keep costs under control, skimping on key people is a big mistake. If you have a growth mindset, you are willing to pay a market-competitive price to bring in a significant hire who can help the business expand.

- **Settling for competence.** Here, entrepreneurs believe that anyone with adequate skills can do the job, seeking competence when they should be striving for greatness. Entrepreneurs need at least some employees capable of going beyond competence, who are motivated to take good risks, to test innovative ideas, to work zealously to achieve stretch goals. But if you're thinking only in terms of competence, you're not going to attract potential high achievers in your recruiting efforts.

- **Failing to sell the company to top candidates.** Entrepreneurs usually are excellent salespeople, but of ideas, products, and services rather than their companies. With the Myth of Smallness dominating their perspective, they don't court top candidates; they don't communicate their vision for the company with passion and eloquence; they don't make a convincing case that a highly talented individual should leave a good job for a potentially great one.

- **Choosing control over profit.** In *The Founder's Dilemmas*, Noam Wasserman distinguishes between people who are motivated by control versus profit. Entrepreneurs under the influence of this myth tend to choose control over profit. They prefer the security of smallness, of having control over every aspect of a business instead of ceding control to others in order to grow and become more successful. Therefore, they hire people who they know they can control rather than individuals who are leaders and who are willing to voice ideas and take the company in directions that are different from the companies' founders.

The Myth of Greatness Mistakes

- **Winging it.** When entrepreneurs are overconfident without cause, they believe they can spot a great hire instantly and instinctively. As a result, they lack a process for identifying which candidate would be a good fit for the company, both in terms of skills and values.

- **Bringing in the clones.** Many entrepreneurs hire people who possess similar backgrounds, personalities, and interests as themselves. These entrepreneurs want to surround themselves with like-minded employees, people who are fun to be around and who make good first impressions. The entrepreneurs have big egos, so they want employees who are chips off the old block.

This is the fraternity president style of hiring, where the "cool kids" are offered membership and the freaks and geeks are excluded. This is very different from hiring people who share similar values, since people can have the same beliefs and mission as an entrepreneur but have wildly different personalities and ways of working.

- **Paying too much for too little.** Convinced that huge success is around the corner, some entrepreneurs don't mind spending a lot of money for a key hire. The problem: They're buying reputation and skills rather than fit. They may get someone who is excellent at a given set of tasks, but if the fit isn't there, the hire may leave after a short tenure. Even worse, if he stays, he may create morale problems because his style may clash with the company culture.

- **Failing to search long and deep enough.** Impatience is a problem for entrepreneurs who perceive greatness when they're far from it. They feel and act like CEOs of Fortune 100 companies, and as a result, they expect everything to happen immediately. For this reason, they don't take the time to seek out, assess, and spend time with job candidates. They choose the first person who strikes their fancy rather than waiting for the person who is right for the job.

COUNTERACTING THE MYTH EFFECT

Awareness of these myths goes a long way toward preventing them from damaging the recruiting process. Awareness alone isn't enough, however. I've worked with entrepreneurs who are aware that their sense of smallness or greatness is affecting their decisions as leaders, and as much as they may resolve not to let their ingrained viewpoints shape their actions, their resolution can diminish over time.

Therefore, let me offer you some suggestions that will help you counteract the power of these myths, first for the Myth of Smallness:

Calculate the value of a great hire in a key position. I've found that entrepreneurs are willing to spend money to hire great people when they recognize how much value—both directly and indirectly—those hires can add to their companies. Rather than commoditize the labor function, they should attach value to hiring the right person for the job.

To illustrate how this is done, consider a conversation I had with a CEO of a small tech company that was going through a rapid growth period. At the time, his payroll was $5 million, and he was concerned that if he overpaid for the new managers and specialists he needed based on their growth spurt, he might jeopardize the company's future. I responded, "Let's say your worst fears come true, and we overpay everyone we hire by 20 percent and your payroll goes up to $6 million. What value might you obtain in return if they're the right people for the job?" Here's the value we calculated:

- Increased productivity by 10 percent or more, often exponentially
- Fewer management problems because of their fit with the culture
- Increased enjoyment being CEO (because a better fit means fewer conflicts and problems)
- Increased revenue by at least 15 percent because of better expertise and opportunities to use this expertise (people perform better when they are in synch with company work style and values)

A few years later, after making the hires we recommended, this CEO sold his company for $800 million based on $25 million in revenues—more than two and a half times the multiple on a publicly traded, SaaS enterprise business at the time. This was in large part due to the investment in getting "top of the market" people he brought into his company.

Pitch the company to candidates like you pitched your products and services to customers. Most entrepreneurs have natural sales ability, but too often, they aren't involved directly in the recruitment process or they are involved but fail to communicate their vision with power and passion. It may seem odd to some entrepreneurs to do this sort of thing—after all, you may think "I'm the buyer here, not the seller"—but sometimes, this is the only way you'll be able to convince a top candidate to join your company. Candidates need to feel a kinship with you, a belief in what you're trying to accomplish and feel that there's a natural affinity between themselves and your mission. When they feel that, they'll have trouble saying no.

Be willing to hire people who know more—or different things—than you do. If you're thinking small, this is a scary suggestion. You lose a measure of control when you become dependent on someone else to help the company grow and prosper. At the same, you gain an invaluable resource for the company, both today and in the future. If you want to scale and grow, you probably need at least one person who has done what you haven't, who can fill in the knowledge blanks. Most entrepreneurs I know love to learn—to master new areas of the business. Think of the person you hire as not just an employee, but as a teacher. As much as the new hire can learn from you, you also can learn a lot from her.

Here's how to counteract the Greatness Myth's effects on hiring:

Focus on execution. More specifically, vow to hire people who are brilliant at getting things done rather than those who look great on paper, possess great bravado, and seem like they're smarter than everyone else. Some people talk a good game and others possess terrific track records and reputations, but entrepreneurs much more so than big corporations need people who can meet deadlines, implement strategies, and achieve stretch goals. Don't be impressed as much by personal style or how someone presents himself as by his ability to execute. When you interview candidates, ask them about how they managed to accomplish a difficult objective—what they did to make sure they achieved it. Note if they talk about how they cut red tape or found shortcuts around policies and procedures to get things done. In every company, there's someone who understands how to work the company's system—how to speed up processes, how to spot and correct mistakes, and so on. Of course, make sure their shortcuts and other execution tactics were ethical, safe, and legal. A big difference exists between finding ingenious ways to get things done versus taking shortcuts that expose a company to lawsuits, that expose people to harm, or that are morally wrong.

Emphasize candidate diversity. Don't get locked into only interviewing people who have MBAs from top programs or who have worked for prestigious consulting firms. There's nothing wrong with any of those credentials, but you want to make sure that you're not ruling out people who would be great for the job except they lack a singular credential. Be entrepreneurial in your hiring—be open-minded, creative, willing to take a risk. Consider a range of candidates before making your choice.

Recognize that there's more than one great candidate out there.
I know an owner of a fast-growing retail business who was smitten with an executive vice president of a large corporation who at a conference had expressed interest in joining an entrepreneurial company. As this owner's business grew, he became convinced that this guy was the one and only person who could help him take his company to the next level. When he offered him the job, though, the guy said it was a bad time for him to leave and he turned down the offer. The owner was devastated and couldn't muster the energy to interview anyone else, turning the hiring process over to an assistant who proceeded to make a mediocre hire.

Over eight years ago, I made my first placement as an independent executive recruiter. An advertising technology company had raised $8 million for a travel-related startup, and they needed to hire a sales leader. They needed someone who understood the intricate metrics of digital marketing, and so we focused on finding someone from Google, since they had a deserved reputation for employing salespeople who were highly analytical and could communicate about digital marketing to CMOs. We had a thirty-day window to find and hire someone, and on day twenty-eight we made an offer to a Google executive. Though we had assumed he would take the job, he told us his wife didn't want him to leave Google, so he turned us down. But we had other Google sales executives in the candidate pipeline who were also finalists for the position, and we called one of them. Not only was he as good as the person we initially offered the job to, but he turned out to be an even better fit: His values matched those of the startup founders, he was great at closing deals but also at growing his own people (a critical cultural requirement), and his style of working blended perfectly with that of the executive team. He took the job, was there for six years, and helped the company surpass $100 million in sales during that time.

The moral of this story: Don't be discouraged if your first choice turns you down. There are other candidates out there who will be excellent, but you may have to dig deeper and wait a bit longer to find them.

A REAL OPTION FOR EITHER MYTH

At a certain point in the lives of their companies, entrepreneurs need to make a crucial hire. Typically, it's at a point where the company is on the cusp of significant growth, and the founders realize they need to find someone who has capabilities beyond those that any of their existing employees possess. This is when they need to get serious about Level 3 recruiting, since odds are that the person they seek isn't in their network. Myth of Greatness entrepreneurs are likely to choose the candidate with the most impressive resume, feeling that this is the right match for their incredible company. Myth of Smallness entrepreneurs are likely to choose the most affordable candidate who also has the experience and expertise the job requires.

Both groups of entrepreneurs, however, are likely to be blinded by competence. More specifically, they won't assess for values because they are so concerned about a candidate's capabilities. Again, I'm not suggesting these capabilities are of no significance. But values are crucial for long-term productivity and success, and both myths direct people toward technical competence. The small myth entrepreneur thinks, "I've got to compromise between a person I can afford and a person who will be able to do this job effectively." The greatness myth entrepreneur thinks, "I deserve the best of the best, the smartest and most competent person available."

How can you refocus attention on values? Here's a simple

technique I've used over the years that helps:

1. List five people you've worked with over the years who you enjoyed working with and who performed well within your company and culture.
2. Identify three out of the five with whom you resonated the strongest, who seemed to be attuned to your goals and beliefs.
3. Name the values these individuals shared.
4. Determine if candidates for important positions also possess these values.

Using this method will help you avoid compromising on values. It's fine to compromise on technical chops—to take someone who may lack a certain amount of experience because she is a high-potential hire who might grow with the company or an individual who is burning to learn a new skill. But values are a non-negotiable. In fact, you want people who not only fit with your values but who can amplify them. Make the effort to interview people and search for their beliefs and motivations. What are their hopes and dreams, their goals for the future? Once you know their core values, you can not only determine if they fit your organization but you can create a vision for them of what their career and life will be like if they accept your offer. In this way, you can convince them that greatness is attainable within your company, and this more than anything else will convince them to sign on.

CHAPTER 4

Evangelical Zeal
and a SEAL
Team's Focus

One of the books I most admire about executive search is *Topgrading* by Bradford Smart. I respect it because Smart demonstrates why talent selection is a business priority rather than "only" an HR function. Smart's emphasis on hiring A players for key positions and eliminating C players is powerful; he makes a convincing case for a company's success being linked with its ability to find and hire A players as much (or more than) creating great products and business strategies.

This book, though, was written in 1999 and came out in 2000 when the economy was in a trough and many qualified candidates existed for every position. Back then, selection was crucial. Today, when the vast majority of top candidates are employed—and often employed by great companies—recruitment is far more important than selection. Moreover, it comes before selection.

Recruiting and extracting great candidates from great companies is as much art as science. This is the challenge entrepreneurs face today. All the advice I've offered—making recruiting a priority; using a tried-and-true process to identify, extract, and secure qualified candidates (rather than winging it); finding a core values fit between candidate and company—will be for naught if you don't bring two qualities to the process: evangelical zeal and a SEAL team's focus. Let's start out by defining what these qualities entail.

YOU CAN'T EXTRACT IF YOU'RE LAID BACK

When I've spoken to founders and other entrepreneurial leaders about the need for them to be involved and engaged in the recruitment process, they nod and say of course. When I describe what this involvement and engagement entails, however, some of them have second thoughts. As one owner of a small retail business said, "You mean I have to spend all that time assessing, interviewing, and selling all the serious candidates?" As much as most entrepreneurs want to meet people who are applying for important positions in their companies and have the final say about who gets hired, they are taken aback not only by the time required but the need for both intellectual and emotional engagement.

When I talk about evangelical zeal, I'm referring to an entrepreneur's willingness to plunge deeply into the recruiting process and approach job candidates as sellers rather than buyers. More specifically, it means:

- Engaging in conversations, assessment, and reflection to determine if there's a fit between a candidate and the company
- Making the effort to determine which candidate is best for the long-term mission, not just the short-term requirements of the job

■ Selling the candidates on the company with honesty, eloquence, and passion

Understandably, some entrepreneurs never thought of their role as involving all these tasks. They prefer their roles as moneymakers and business strategists. They claim not to have much interest or experience in recruitment and selection. Unfortunately, if they are dispassionate observers of the recruitment process or just want to make the final selection, they will end up choosing a mediocre candidate or one who may be worse than mediocre.

While some recruiting tasks can be delegated—and in larger entrepreneurial companies there needs to be recruiting competency at all levels—no one else grasps the company's essence like you. Even more important, no one else will do as good a job as you of convincing a candidate for a top position to join your company. Most important of all, no one else has as much skin in the game: You're the one who's likely to think longest, hardest, and most astutely about who will help you achieve your objectives, especially if you're hiring for a senior management position. In the words of Irv Grousbeck, "you can hire people to do anything, except hire people."

So an entrepreneur's ability to be all in with this process—to spend the time, make the effort, and sell the prospect—is crucial for a successful hire.

STRIKE HARD AND WITH PRECISION

You can't take a laissez faire approach or only have a vague idea of what you're looking for in a candidate and expect to make a successful hire. Not only won't you identify the right group of candidates, but even if you manage to do so through dumb luck, you won't be able to convince the right one to join your organization.

Navy SEAL teams are so effective because they strike with great force based on great planning. They are incredibly well prepared, and this enables them to hit targets with surgical precision. Think about this analogy in terms of recruitment. You can approach your "target" without much thought and planning or even certainty that it's the right target; or you can zoom in with a well-conceived strategy and extract him quickly and powerfully.

Entrepreneurs may be fly-by-the-seat-of-their-pants people, but they can master this latter approach if they're motivated; they need to believe that filling a given position is a critical task for the future of their company. When they're so motivated, they put in the time and thought necessary to identify the right candidates, and they create a sales pitch that will convince the right candidates to join their company.

Marty was an advertising entrepreneur who created a small, independent ad agency in Chicago years ago. Marty was the quintessential instinctive businessman who said whatever was on his mind and built his ad agency without much planning, relying on his networking and sales skills to bring in small, entrepreneurial clients. After about ten years of growth, the business plateaued. Marty realized that if he wanted to realize his vision for the agency—to be the largest and best agency in the niche in which he operated—he needed to hire someone who could bring in better clients, upgrade creative efforts, and run the company more efficiently. Driven to find this individual, Marty created a list of traits he was searching for that combined competencies with softer, less easily defined abilities. He wanted someone who had experience with and contacts among Fortune 500 companies, but he also required an individual who believed in creating a family-oriented culture.

Armed with his list, Marty treated it with Bible-like reverence, refusing to deviate from it despite temptations to do so. He rejected candidates who possessed great selling ability but didn't share his beliefs about how an ad agency should be run. Finally, he found George, a young but dynamic account supervisor at a much larger ad agency. George met all the criteria for the position, but Marty recognized it would be an uphill battle to convince him to leave a much bigger agency and accept a lower salary. Yet he was absolutely convinced that he had found the ideal person. During their meeting, Marty explained why he believed the agency could quadruple in size over the next ten years if he recruited an executive vice president who possessed certain skills and beliefs about running a business—skills and beliefs that Marty said George possessed. He asked George where he wanted to be in ten years, and George explained that he hoped to be the CEO of a highly successful ad agency that felt like family. At that point, Marty showed George the list of skills and qualities he had created, and when George saw it, he nodded and accepted the position. Ten years later, George was the CEO and they had quintupled their billings.

MOTIVATE YOURSELF FOR ZEAL AND SEAL

In many ways, Marty was a typical entrepreneur. He was an instinctive risk-taker, and he would have been the first one to admit that he didn't spend much time on recruiting and hiring tasks. He would have also said that when he was involved in these areas, he tried to hire the most technically qualified candidate for the least money possible.

So Marty, like many entrepreneurs, didn't bring evangelical zeal or a SEAL team's precision and drive to recruiting naturally. It was only when he realized how high the stakes were that he approached the process with a laser-like focus and was able to make a powerful argument to sway the candidate he targeted.

To help you adopt the zeal and SEAL-like drive necessary to recruit effectively, here are some motivational tips:

- **The candidate you want isn't sitting on the couch eating chips and waiting for the phone to ring.** Odds are, the best candidate has a terrific job and may be hiding in plain sight. So you have to put in the effort to find her and then make a great pitch to convince her to join your company. Otherwise, you're going to end up hiring someone who may be competent but will fail to help you achieve significant objectives.

- **Dabblers regret their dabbling.** It's like home repair. You may like fooling around with small projects, like installing a new light switch. But if it's something major, like rewiring the entire house, then you'll regret the outcome—burning down the place—if you're a dabbler. In recruiting, you may be able to get away with an amateurish approach for less-significant positions, but for key ones, dabbling can burn down the business.

- **True believers deliver great value.** Most entrepreneurs, whether they're running high-powered tech startups or smaller, no-tech service businesses, recognize the importance of surrounding themselves with people who share their vision; who believe in what the founder is trying to accomplish and the way he is trying to accomplish it. Cynics and skeptics and egomaniacs, on the other hand, thwart this vision, intentionally or not. Therefore, you want to bring in people who believe in your methods and objectives. There's no way to know if they're true believers, however, unless you enmesh yourself in the hiring process and target your candidate with precision.

FOCUS ON THE WHY

Here's an analogy that always provides me with renewed motivation. Three laborers are breaking stones in the hot sun. The first one is miserable, complaining that he's hot and thirsty and all he's doing is this menial job of swinging his hammer and breaking up rocks into smaller pieces. The second one isn't complaining, since he's glad to have a job and able to put food on the table, but he's not going about his task with much energy or enthusiasm. The third laborer, however, is ecstatic about his task and breaks up more stones than the two other laborers combined. When asked why he is happy and productive, he responds, "Because I'm building a temple."

The third laborer knows something instinctively that most of us have to learn. Simon Sinek, marketing expert and author of *Start with Why*, gave a TED talk that addresses this point. Sinek tells us that great leaders communicate not by talking about what or how but start with the *why*.

Great communicators focus on the *why* of their audience. Why do they get up every day and do what they do? What is their overarching purpose? This is why selling a candidate on the position by focusing on the money bottom line is like trying to sell a product by talking about . . . the product. "We make great cars." Or "We make great computers." Working for a paycheck is a *what*. It's a result, an endgame.

The rational part of the brain might like these messages well enough. But they aren't messages that get people in the gut. But start with the why—the source of their drive, their passion, their motivation—and you reach people where it really matters.

Ever try to get a confirmed "Mac person" to switch brands? If you have, you'll know it's a losing proposition . . . and you'll get a glimpse of the power of starting with the *why*.

The why is also the right place to start when you pitch your company to the right candidate. Explain why you get up in the morning. Why you built this business. Why you think it makes a difference in the world to be doing what you do.

As Sinek puts it: "If you hire people just because they can do a job, they'll work for your money, but if they believe what you believe, they'll work for you with blood and sweat and tears."

A STUDY IN CONTRASTS

To clarify the difference between the approach I'm advocating versus the less zealous and unfocused method used by some entrepreneurs, here's a chart listing the contrasting traits of each:

ZEAL-AND-SEAL

- ▶ Creates a plan/strategy to find the right candidates for a key job
- ▶ Identifies both the tangible (skills) and intangible (values) qualities essential for the job
- ▶ Is involved continuously and directly in the process; knows exactly how it's progressing, offers input, communicates with candidates and helps assess each one
- ▶ Cares more about the quality of the search than about getting it done as quickly as possible
- ▶ Acts as the closer when a candidate is chosen; makes the pitch to the candidate to join the company, painting a picture that helps the candidate see the values fit
- ▶ Conducts a post-recruitment debrief regularly, assessing what went right and wrong in the search, thereby building a database to learn from and improve the process

PASSIVE AND UNFOCUSED

- ▶ Pursues candidates in an ad hoc and at times random and disorganized manner

- ▶ Relies exclusively on the job specs to guide the search

- ▶ Is involved sporadically in the search, asking others who are more directly involved how it's going and becoming more involved when the schedule permits (or others tell him he needs to be more involved)

- ▶ Is obsessed about finding a qualified candidate immediately

- ▶ Acts as a buyer rather than a seller; expects candidates to recognize the opportunity rather than describing the opportunity in compelling detail

The passive and unfocused approach is easier and often quicker, which makes it appealing to stressed-out entrepreneurs. In the *sturm und drang* of daily business life, filling a key position as fast as possible feels like an imperative—problems seem to pile up every day the position is still open. I know that an unfilled job can hang like a Damoclean Sword above entrepreneurs' heads, tempting them to forget about their recruitment strategy or to use compensation as the primary tool to convince someone to take the job.

But think of all the times you've regretted acting impulsively or without a plan, or how you've beaten yourself up because your lack of involvement resulted in a missed opportunity. Whether these actions involved recruiting or some other aspect of the business, it probably produced an unfavorable outcome.

Let's take a look at some specific situations that will illustrate the value of evangelical zeal and a SEAL team's focus.

SITUATION #1

FALLING IN LOVE AT FIRST SIGHT

Carrie runs a profitable catering company that specializes in high-end dinners for small, intimate gatherings. She's been in business for three years and though it was a struggle initially, she has a good network of loyal customers and has built her company through referrals. Carrie is a good promoter and is perceptive about people—she found a terrific chef who she was able to hire at a reasonable salary because he didn't have a lot of experience, and she also has been astute in her other hires. But to help her company continue to grow, she has decided she must expand into a new market sector. Carrie does some research and sees an opportunity to cater business functions, but she has few contacts in this sector. She decides to hire a salesperson with this experience and expertise, bringing in a local search firm to help her find the right person. But before she can do so, she has lunch with a friend who tells Carrie that her sister, Laura, has been working in sales for a huge Fortune 100 company in another city. Now Laura is interested in moving back to where she grew up and doing something more entrepreneurial and would be willing to work on commission.

Carrie meets Laura for coffee and is tremendously impressed. Though Laura doesn't have contacts in the local business community and her sales experience is limited to the software industry, she is an attractive, dynamic presence and loves food—they talk about their favorite recipes for much of the time they're together. The next day, Carrie calls Laura and offers her the job, convinced that she's found the ideal person to help her expand the business.

In fact, Laura turns out to be a disaster. Her lack of contacts in the local business community present problems, but even worse, Laura and Carrie aren't on the same wavelength when it comes to the business. For Laura, this is just a "fun" diversion until she finds something more meaningful; she isn't willing to put in the long hours building a base of contacts or learn the business. She tends to talk down to prospective customers, viewing them as not as significant professionally as the people she dealt with when she was working for the Fortune 100 company. After less than a year, she quits before Carrie can fire her, taking a job with a large corporation.

If Carrie had possessed more SEAL-like focus and a well-conceived plan for finding a salesperson, she would not have been seduced by Laura's charm and Fortune 100 sales experience. She would not have fallen in love at first sight.

Too often, entrepreneurs "confabulate" the greatness of candidates who make good first impressions. Because many small business owners like acting quickly, decisively, and instinctively, they often meet a job candidate who appears perfect for the position. They are impatient and don't want to look a gift horse in the mouth, so rather than going through the process and relying on a dynamic strategy and their own intense involvement to produce the right person for the job, they convince themselves that they're extraordinarily lucky and fate has given them the ideal candidate.

In these situations, entrepreneurs must remind themselves to trust their process rather than their instinctive first reactions. When they hire the first person who they interview, they often hire the wrong person. SEAL teams have tremendous discipline: Entrepreneurs need to exhibit the same steel will and resist grabbing the first person who makes a good impression.

"Hire slow. Fire fast." That's how Stanford University business professor and entrepreneurial expert Irving Grousbeck puts it. It's the same advice relationship experts give: Don't get married after the first date. You may feel pressure to hire someone to fill a critical position, but try to take it as slowly as is feasible. Once you determine that a candidate is a good fit from a values and mission standpoint, then hire her. It may take you a little more time than normal to make this determination, but you'll be much less likely to fire the person you hire within the year. And, having alternative candidates is likely to produce a better result.

If you do make this mistake and hire the wrong person, don't allow your hubris or rationalizations to get in the way of recognizing your mistake and firing this individual. Liza Landsman, former chief marketing officer of E*Trade Financial and current president of Jet.com, said that one key lesson in hiring she learned early on was that "often the greatest hiring mistakes one makes are not firing the wrong people soon enough." Landsman recalled a member of a team she led early in her career who was really talented on paper, but who didn't have the chemistry, culture, or mindset to flourish on the team. Landsman kept trying to fix the situation.

"I just kept thinking, it's a failure of leadership," she said. "She needs coaching, she needs support, she needs feedback. The whole team needs to support her. And what I really failed to realize is that her negativity was incredibly infectious, and it was harming the productivity, not just of her as an individual, but of the entire team."

Eventually another member of the team confronted Landsman about the situation.

"It was a real wake-up call to me that the right decision too late has very little value," Landsman said. "And, so that's something I really think of, both in hiring—looking at that cultural fit, and not just skill set fit—but . . . recognizing when people are either on the wrong team or in the wrong job, and moving much more swiftly [to remedy the situation], because it breeds less negativity that way."

SITUATION #2
THE BEST CANDIDATE HAS A BETTER JOB

Daniel launched his Silicon Valley startup, and one of his first actions was to hire a staff of ten. Of the ten positions he planned to fill, Daniel was focused on one in particular—chief financial officer. Daniel was a tech guy, and he was brilliant at programming and highly creative, but when it came to finances, he was uninterested at best, incompetent at worst. To his credit, he knew this was a weakness, and he also recognized that to realize his long-term goals, he had to have someone who was astute about everything from budgeting with the limited funds available to scaling the company in a financially feasible manner to going public (his ultimate goal).

Daniel, who had a healthy ego, targeted a number of top financial executives who worked for major Silicon Valley companies. Five of them came in for interviews, and Daniel decided to offer the job to one of the candidates—but he turned down the offer. Daniel moved on to the second candidate he liked, but he too said no. Both of them admired Daniel's startup concept and his track record, but they didn't want to go from one of the top companies in the Valley to one that had just launched and whose future was still uncertain.

Anticipating that some of the candidates would be reluctant to leave big companies for a startup, Daniel had sought to impress them by emphasizing his accomplishments working for other companies as well as a previous successful startup; he also talked about how the CFO would receive a salary that was even more than Daniel's compensation and that he would have equity in the company. But what he failed to discuss was how he believed in a participatory, inclusive culture; how he wanted to create a company that was a hybrid of a family business and a typical tech company; how he believed the company could not only shake up the industry but provide a product that might change people's lives.

With the third candidate, Daniel spoke from the heart. He was authentic and engaged as he shared his vision, and he was up-front about the obstacles and how he hoped to overcome them. He was clear about his desire to create a different type of company, one that didn't just make a lot of money but could really make a difference.

This candidate accepted, admitting he was taking a chance by doing so but saying he was willing to risk failure for the dream that Daniel described.

Learn Daniel's lesson. If you play the dispassionate professional—or, even worse, remove yourself from the interviewing process—you probably have no chance of convincing top candidates to switch jobs. You have to be involved, genuine, and articulate about your company and its future if you hope to pry a great candidate out of a great job. Evangelical zeal doesn't mean you have to shout from the mountaintops or emote like a character in a soap opera, but it does require you to deliver a compelling pitch. You can preach quietly, but you must do a good job of conveying why making the company successful matters to you and what that success will look like.

SITUATION #3

THE INTERVIEW PROCESS COMES AT A HECTIC TIME

A mid-sized company was searching for a chief technology officer at a tumultuous time in its history. The founder and CEO was in the process of restructuring the company, to make it more profitable as well as to bring more innovation to its product development. The CEO contacted me to help with the recruitment process, and after a long search, we narrowed the candidate list down to two. The CEO scheduled one candidate for a Monday interview, the other for Wednesday. The CEO allotted the same amount of time for each interview, created a list of topics that he wanted to cover with the candidates, and had two other members of his executive team in the interviews.

The Monday meeting with the first candidate went great; she seemed to be highly qualified from a skills standpoint and also possessed the attitude and beliefs that would make her a good fit for the company. The Wednesday meeting, however, was not as good. The candidate had the same sterling credentials, but the CEO and the two members of the executive team didn't get the same positive feeling from this second candidate that they received from the first one.

In reviewing these two interviews with the CEO, I asked if there was anything "external" to the interview itself that might have prejudiced them in favor of the Monday candidate. After some discussion, the CEO said that the Wednesday interview was harder for him and his two colleagues because they had a board meeting scheduled for the next day and they were all scrambling to prepare data for the board about the restructuring. The CEO admitted they were a bit distracted and harried during the second interview. As we discussed this situation, the CEO realized that their response to the second candidate was based much more on their attitude that day rather than the candidate herself. They ended up re-interviewing both candidates and hiring the Wednesday candidate, who so far has worked out great.

The lesson here is to maintain iron discipline from start to finish while going through the recruiting protocols. It's so easy for outside events or personal bias to skew the results of the process without being aware of how they're affecting the process. Therefore, adhere to a recruitment plan assiduously. Remind yourself every step of the way that no matter how chaotic things are, you can't let it affect your recruiting process. If you have a recruiting strategy in place and resolve to stick to it with military discipline, this will help avoid situations like the one just described.

CAPITALIZING ON
THE ZEAL-AND-SEAL OF OTHERS

As critical as it is for you to be involved in the recruitment process, it may not be possible or appropriate for you to be the point person for every new hire, especially if you're a relatively large or growing company. I've worked with a number of entrepreneurs who when they started out were able to make good hiring choices based on their circles of friends and colleagues. As I noted earlier, sometimes hiring a college friend or someone with whom you worked closely early in your career ensures that you're bringing in someone who shares your values. You may not have done a formal analysis of what those values are, but you have learned through experience that they share your sense of mission and workstyle. The problem is that as your business grows, your circle isn't large enough to provide a pool of candidate who possess both the values and skills you require.

Similarly, you may recognize that you need outside help to find the person who would make a big difference. As the head of an executive recruitment firm, I obviously have a certain bias about this topic, but I can tell you objectively that any good firm can increase your ability to find the right candidates and join your company. Entrepreneurs need to be aware, however, that not all recruitment firms are created equal—I'll suggest some guidelines to assist you in finding one that will be effective. First, though, let's address how to make sure you find the right candidate when your company is large or growing and you can't do everything yourself.

The simple solution is making your company a values-driven recruiting organization from the top down. This means training your key people in the principles I've espoused in these pages: understanding the values and mission of the company, targeting candidates who possess both compatible values and skills, recruiting with discipline, strategy, and zeal, selling the company's larger and deeper raison d'être rather than just the job itself. You want your customer service head (as well as all your functional department executives) to be able to hire customer-facing representatives who grasp the long-term goals and cultural norms of the company.

Here's an easy technique to implement this suggestion: Every leader conveys these principles one level down. This is a job requirement for every person in a leadership position. Entrepreneurs should train their leaders in how to do so using the process detailed in chapters 5 through 8. In this way, the philosophy is imbued in managers at different levels and in different functions, spreading this recruiting mindset quickly and effectively.

As founder and TriNet's CEO for the company's first 20 years, Martin Babinec is one of the key entrepreneurs who helped build the industry of professional employer organizations (PEOs). He is a fierce evangelist for establishing and propagating core values. TriNet runs on five core values: Personal Growth, Orientation to the Future, Integrity, Service, and Entrepreneurialism (POISE). Not content to let these core ideals remain static slogans posted on the walls or trotted out in speeches, Babinec integrated them into the company's operational processes. Every significant decision the company makes is reviewed for fit with the five core values and colleagues hold each other accountable to these same values.

Now let's turn to the question of an executive recruiting firm. While many such firms exist, some are bad and some are inappropriate for entrepreneurs. The bad ones will give you a list of candidates who only possess the skills required (with little attention given to the fit between candidate values and work norms and those of the organization). The inappropriate ones are large and aren't able to customize their recruitment process to the needs of small and growing entrepreneurial companies.

With those caveats in mind, here are four tips that will help you choose the right firm to assist you in your recruitment efforts:

- **Determine if the firm has a process in place to understand your culture and core values.** It's not enough to understand the list of competencies you seek in a new executive. Each candidate a headhunter brings you should be vetted for the targeted core value set.

- **Ask who will be leading the search.** Remember the adage: *Success has many fathers, failure is an orphan.* Make sure your search will be led directly by someone whose name is on the door. That way the success or failure of your search will reflect directly on the firm you've brought on board. It's the quickest and best way to ensure accountability—and to avoid having a crucial search languish for months on the desk of an overwhelmed associate.

- **Make sure that the person you work with at a search firm has prior experience as an entrepreneur building a company.** A search executive who has been on the inside, rapidly scaling up both an executive team and the functional teams that support them, will understand your needs and growing pains intuitively.

- **Find a partner who demonstrates the energy, enthusiasm, and engagement critical to selling candidates.** It's one thing to find great candidates who are ideally suited for a job and a company; it's something else entirely to convince them to join the company. Obviously, you can help a search firm sell candidates on your company, but you want a partner who also is adept at convincing people to take a leap of faith. You don't want someone who seems to search by the numbers, who displays little eloquence or verve when describing your company to candidates. You do want someone who is gifted in selling the underlying value and mission of your company, who can describe it in a way that is not only accurate but motivating.

Now you know the overarching philosophy of highly effective entrepreneurial recruiting. This means it's time to move to the next step: Learning the process to implement this philosophy.

CHAPTER 5

Map the Organization's Foundational Mission and Values

The next four chapters focus on the four steps required to put into action the entrepreneurial recruiting mindset covered in the first section of the book. These four steps are mapping your company's mission and values; testing your perceptions of the candidate's strengths and weaknesses, which may be right or wrong; mapping the candidate's mission and values; and finally extracting the best candidates for your company.

Before focusing on the first process step in this chapter, under-stand that the four steps in this section aren't necessarily in chrono-logical order. In real life, you may take these steps simultaneously; or you may implement parts of each step at different times; or you may be in the middle of a search when you discover this book and decide to use its concepts retroactively.

TIME WELL SPENT

No doubt, you may think that the first step is to start searching for candidates, given that what you *want* to do is hire someone, preferably as quickly as possible. But the payoff of taking the time to assess your mission and values is huge. It's what will enable you to make the right match and hire someone who will contribute greatly to your company for a long time.

Still, when you read this chapter's title, you may have reacted with one of the following statements:

What does this have to do with hiring a great employee?

I know our mission and values. I can skip this chapter.

How am I supposed to figure out our missions and values?

As an entrepreneur, you're probably a pragmatist. You largely focus on strategies and tactics, goals and objectives, not the more intangible concepts of mission and values. But even if you recognize the importance of these concepts, you may be operating under certain misconceptions: You may be confusing strategy with mission or best practices with values. It's possible, too, that you possess a vague or not-altogether-accurate idea of what your mission and values are.

None of this is a problem if you put in the time and effort to assess and define your mission and values properly. That's the goal of this chapter. But first, I want to make sure we're clear about our terms.

Mission is how you envision your company a number of years down the road (ten years is a good milepost)—a vision of what you hope your company will achieve. *Values* are how you'll go about turning this mission into reality. And there's a third concept:

personal mission statement. The mission you have for your company must synch with the mission you have for yourself. Entrepreneurs are reflections of their organizations, and if a disconnect exists between what you want for yourself and what you hope your company will become, it's a problem.

To avoid this problem and others when hiring, let's look at how to identify these three crucial elements, starting with mission.

WHAT DO YOU WANT YOUR COMPANY TO BECOME?

Admittedly, this isn't a question that you can necessarily answer off the top of your head. Certainly you know what you want your company to achieve this year in terms of revenue and profits, but mission is larger and longer than that. Think ten years down the road, and think of your company's best, most idealistic evolution. Then answer the following questions:

- How will this vision of your company make the world better (world meaning anything from society at large to the customer base you serve)?
- What problem are you solving (i.e., dealing with a serious environmental issue, creating a service that is faster, better, and cheaper)?
- How much pain (physical harm, monetary loss, frustration with available products) is associated with that problem?
- How much goodness (benefits to various audiences) will solving this problem bring?
- How many people can be served with this solution (hundreds, thousands, millions)?

Some of you may be a bit taken aback by this language. You run a grocery store, a small hardware store chain, a management consulting business, a law firm. Perhaps you've never considered how you're making the world better or how you're taking away people's pain. But when we talk in the context of mission, that's exactly what you're doing. You're making people's lives easier by providing them with a place to buy groceries in a food desert; or you're doing a better job than others of planning people's estates and taking a load off their minds. Remember, this is a mission, a vision, something that you hope to build in the future. By filling in the details of this mission, you gain a better sense of the people who can help you achieve it.

Now let's get more specific about that mission. Answer the following:

- Do you see your company becoming the leader in the category; a mid-level player; a strong niche operator?
- Do you envision your company ten times larger than it is today; five times larger; about the same size?
- In the future, will your company be serving essentially the same customer base; a somewhat more diverse base; a significantly broader base, with new demographics?
- How will the outside world describe your company; will they talk about it as "fast-growing and committed to social issues"; "solid and conservative"; "a great place to work"?
- What will be your point of difference ten years from now, the factor that not only provides you with a competitive edge but that makes you stand out in an increasingly volatile and complex environment?

As you consider these questions, be visionary but don't engage in fantasy. You may have a great little soap company, but if your mission is to usurp Procter & Gamble as market leader in ten years, you're probably not being realistic. Think about what you could become in ten years, given what you've built now and your resources for growth in the future.

Given this mission, what sort of people do you need to help you achieve it? If your vision of the company is one that requires 150 percent growth annually and you want to change a category with revolutionary new products, then you require people who are not only innovative and willing to work with great diligence and commitment, but who want to be part of a paradigm-shifting company. Are you hiring someone who is agile and forward-looking or someone who is set in her ways and focused on the present?

IDENTIFYING VALUES

At the end of Chapter 3, I suggested an exercise to help you think about what your personal values were. Now let's focus on organizational values by adapting that same exercise.

First, gather a small group of trusted executives—perhaps three members of your executive team. Once gathered, the members of the group—including you—should close their eyes and think about the people in their professional lives with whom they've enjoyed working the most and who were most productive in helping achieve a business mission. Each member of the group should write down the qualities exemplified by each individual they think of. It can be anything from transparency to analytical brilliance to creativity. As you can see, I'm defining values broadly—going beyond personal values such as honesty or loyalty into work-related beliefs and abilities. Be careful to focus on values rather than personality traits or personal competencies. You don't want to come up with a list with items on it like "good sense of humor" or "tenacity." Shared values don't preclude diversity of ideas. Indeed, they should accommodate diversity. As Liza Landsman, president of Jet.com, noted, "Diversity of opinion and points of view is, research- and data-based, confirmed to create better outcomes for business." Shared values will help you hash out your disagreements constructively and forge better solutions and strategies.

Second, discuss the values each of you has identified in the first step. It's likely you're going to have a diverse list, and you want to winnow it down to four to six values. To do so, discuss which values will help the company achieve your identified mission.

Third, exercise your authority as CEO to choose the values if you can't achieve consensus as a group. It's quite possible you won't achieve consensus. Theoretically, any value can be construed as useful for achieving a given mission. If your mission is to create a new healthcare product that provides superior treatment for a disease symptom, you could argue that great integrity is necessary or people might cut corners and violate healthcare regulatory statutes. Someone else might argue that integrity isn't nearly as important as the ability to innovate—that thinking outside the box will be necessary to create a superior treatment product.

Fourth, rank the values in terms of their ability to achieve the company's mission. Determine which one is most critical, which one is second, and so on. Rely on your gut as much as your head. As the CEO, you are the person most familiar with your company's mission and what you need to do to achieve it. If it strikes you that the ability to manage and work on teams is crucial to your particular mission, rank it high. If a value seems useful but dispensable, rank it lower.

Tina founded an environmentally conscious hair care products company and had achieved profitability relatively quickly, selling her products to select retail establishments as well as through online strategies. Tina's goal was to grow the company into related but distinct personal care product markets—skin care, toothpaste, and so on—with a focus on environmental factors. The mission was to become the leading private company in this space, selling their products directly to consumers. When Tina and her team met to define the values they wanted in people, two of her executives lobbied for creativity, believing that they would need to come up with many ideas in the coming years for new products. Though Tina agreed this was an important quality, she deemed it far less important than other values, such as "gumption." Tina believed that for the company to realize its mission, they would need people who were willing to take chances, willing to have the courage of their convictions, and willing to fail.

PERSONAL MISSION STATEMENT

This third element is the one that's most often overlooked. Yet it's crucial, given that entrepreneurs are often strong personalities who start businesses for reasons that go beyond wanting to make money. Typically, they possess their own personal drivers that may be aligned with their organizational missions—or may not. For this reason, identifying that personal mission and assessing its alignment is necessary.

Let me give you an example of one well-known entrepreneur's personal mission. Steve Johnson was the chief revenue officer at Hootsuite, and while there he helped build the social media management company from a valuation of under $100 million to over $1 billion, and from twenty-seven employees to over eight hundred. Steve developed his personal mission at age seventeen when he was working on a farm in Zambia. As Johnson became immersed in daily life in Zambia, he observed that one company had a lock on the shoe market, and that company was charging, per pair, about what the average Zambian worker made in a month.

Realizing this, Johnson got together with some skilled guys he knew on the farm, and they set about figuring out how to make shoes better, faster, and cheaper. He knew he was maneuvering into an important market niche, but more than that, his work was fueled by a sense of purpose, of personal mission.

Many years later, Johnson sums up his philosophy this way: "Purpose drives passion, passion drives engagement and engagement drives productivity."

As a result, Johnson seeks work that allows him to follow his sense of personal mission; he knows that when his personal and company mission are aligned, he will be highly productive.

Assess your own personal mission and how it aligns with your business purpose and goals by doing the following:

Reflect on what you want to achieve with your life via your career. Be specific and honest. Think about what would provide you with great satisfaction and meaning if you could attain it. Again, be realistic, but at the same time, aim high. Who do you dream of being professionally? What are you attempting to become through learning and growth?

Here are some examples of personal mission statements that might facilitate creating your own:

- I want to be the world's best small business marketer.
- I hope to create at least one breakthrough product that revolutionizes our industry.
- I am intent on building a business that is sustainable and that my children can take over.

- I want to create products that make the world a better place to live.
- I am driven to create a company that is more employee-centric, more diverse, and more successful than our competitors.

Assess how your personal mission statement synchs with the organizational mission and accompanying values. For instance, your personal mission statement is: *I want to become a successful innovator in the healthcare space.* To achieve this personal mission, you will need to take risks and follow a steep learning curve; you will also need to be highly creative in an industry overflowing with innovative minds. Your organizational mission, however, might be *to build a successful niche healthcare business*; the values you embrace may include loyalty and perseverance.

As you can guess, this personal mission statement isn't well-aligned with the organizational mission and values. Your personal mission is much more ambitious than the organizational one. You'll probably be frustrated given the gap between the two. Similarly, values such as ambition and creativity are probably more relevant to your personal mission than loyalty and perseverance.

Because of this misalignment, you're likely to hire the wrong people, whether you opt to hire based on either mission. You need to rethink and perhaps readjust what it is you want personally and what it is you want organizationally. You may have misidentified one or you may need to pursue a different entrepreneurial endeavor that is more in line with your personal mission.

Many times, all that's required is tinkering with how you've articulated your mission and values. It may be that your organizational mission was stated too narrowly, or it lacks sufficient ambition. It may be that your corresponding values were a bit off. By articulating your personal mission, you have a chance to correct the company's mission and values and ensure that you hire people who fit with what you really want to achieve down the road.

USE A BLUEPRINT
TO KEEP TRACK OF POTENTIAL FIT

It may seem like a simple thing, but recording missions and values on paper (or electronically) is essential. Recruiting and hiring can be stressful processes, and in this crucible your resolve to use mission and values as a filter may waver or even be forgotten. It's also possible that you try to use them but you find it difficult to translate the mission and values you espouse into best hiring practices—you're fuzzy on whether a given candidate's mission and values jibe with your own.

Therefore, use the following blueprint on the facing page to facilitate mission/values fit.

As you can see, there's a space for you to list the mission and values you identified. Below that, you'll see boxes for core competencies, success factors, and strategic outcomes. Focus on the success factors and see if you can translate the mission and values into candidate traits that will help the organization reach your objectives and that are consistent with the way you want to reach those objectives.

For instance, let's say that your mission is to be a disruptive innovator in the pharmaceutical business, and the values you've targeted include risk-taking and collaboration. You can use the blueprint to link a candidate's personality traits and expressed beliefs with the values you seek. If you ask a candidate if he's collaborative, he will probably say yes. But think a bit more deeply about why you want this value and how it will help you achieve your mission. Is it

CORE FIT SELECTION™

BLUEPRINT

◇◇ DAVE PARTNERS

POSITION [   ]   **DATE** [   ]

COMPANY

MISSION
(What We Are Doing)

CORE VALUES
(Who We Are)

CULTURE
*(How We Do It,
What We Celebrate,
Reward & Recognize)*

ROLE

CORE COMPETENCIES	SUCCESS FACTORS	STRATEGIC OUTCOMES
1.	1.	1.
2.	2.	2.
3.	3.	3.
4.	4.	4.
5.	5.	5.

What are the Intrinsic Qualities This Person Must Possess To Be Effective?	What Must This Person Achieve To Help Drive The Strategic Outcomes?	What Are The Corporate Priorities To Be Achieved In The Next 12 Months?

CANDIDATE

Proven Experience: What Must They Have Already Achieved In Their Career & Bring To This Role?

Must Haves:	Nice To Haves:
1.	1.
	2.
2.	3.
	4.
3.	

Supervisor Name:_____ Title:_____ Signature:_____
(Who Does This Position Report To?)

Copyright 2016 Dave Partners, LLC.   To download more copies and get help implementing these tools, please visit www.HireSmartFromTheStart.com

Go to www.HireSmartFromTheStart.com to download this PDF, instructional videos, and other resources.

because an executive in this position needs to join high-functioning, fast-moving teams and hit the ground running? Is it because you want someone who can deal with the contentious personalities on the team? Is it because your biggest customer is difficult and you need someone who can work well with her from a position of strength? Is it because you need someone who can interact productively with adversaries—regulators, consumer activist groups—and form viable, ongoing relationships with them?

Asking these questions helps you tease out how a value might manifest itself in behaviors. One candidate may tell you a story about how well he works with people he likes; another candidate may tell you a story about how well she works with people who have opposing points of view. If you have a company of contrarians and need someone to collaborate on a diverse, contentious team, this latter person may be the best choice.

Even before you begin the recruitment process, it's worthwhile to speculate about the type of person you're looking for given the identified values and mission. Brainstorm around each value, speculating on the type of personality that might possess a particular value.

Let's say transparency is a key value for your company, since your mission is to become an alternative healthcare insurance broker, capitalizing on a post-Affordable Care Act marketplace. To gain credibility in this marketplace as it evolves, you need to be completely honest and transparent in all your communications, both internally and externally. As a result, you want to hire people who believe in openness and honesty, and who have no hidden agendas. But how does that value translate into a candidate's behaviors?

To make this assessment, think about the various forms transparency can take in workplace behaviors:

- **Relentless honesty.** This person speaks his mind without a filter, offending some people when he says exactly what he is thinking.

- **Truth without considering consequences.** Here, transparency is maintained even when potentially sensitive information is disseminated via social or traditional media; this individual admits that the company is considering a merger with a big insurance company when interviewed by a *New York Times* reporter.

- **Selective openness.** Recognizes that there are certain times when it's judicious to be opaque rather than transparent—i.e., in dealing with the media. In a culture of transparency, this person may be criticized for her selective approach.

- **Transparent in word but not always in deed.** This individual talks honestly and openly to all stakeholders and is willing to admit flaws and failings. Sometimes, however, he'll take actions designed to satisfy agendas known only to himself or a few key people.

Many behavioral permutations exist around every value. By thinking about these permutations and the ones that align with your culture and mission, you are prepared to assess candidates who will represent a spectrum of traits.

USE CULTURE TO DOUBLE CHECK FIT

Speaking of culture, many entrepreneurs are well-versed in their cultures, especially if their companies have been around for a while. Articulating values may be a challenge, but talking about the working environment of their companies is often far easier.

If you're struggling to identify your values, you can use your culture's norms to help surface them. Culture is all about how things are done in your company; and they reflect what is valued, rewarded, and celebrated and what is not.

In one small, family-owned business—a printing company that's been in business for eighty years—the culture prizes people who display loyalty, a willingness to work long hours (a frequent occurrence in the printing business where deadline jobs can require late nights), and an egalitarian attitude.

In a Silicon Valley startup, the culture is quite different. Loyalty is not particularly important (it's assumed many employees will job-hop), while the people who get ahead are those who think out of the box, take risks, and make measurable contributions. In this company's culture, elitism exists and though people work hard, they do it on their own terms and on their own schedules.

As you can imagine, an arrogant-though-brilliant executive would not fit in the family business, and a friendly, conservative conformist wouldn't make it at the Silicon Valley startup.

In real life, of course, it's usually not this black and white. A candidate may mask his arrogance; the friendly conformist may not realize how conservative her decision making is. That's why it helps if you can think about who will fit into your culture before you start the recruiting process. To facilitate this assessment, consider your company's reward and recognition system. Why do people receive raises, promotions, bonuses, and favorable assignments? Look at the following list and make a check next to the reasons that apply to your company:

- ☐ Straight talk
- ☐ Playing politics
- ☐ Seniority
- ☐ Hard work
- ☐ Consensus building
- ☐ Loyalty
- ☐ Teamwork
- ☐ Individual contributions

- [ ] Disruptive innovation
- [ ] Managerial ability/leadership
- [ ] Risk taking
- [ ] Building relationships (with customers and other external groups)
- [ ] Developing people

Use this list not only to assess who will be a good values fit for your culture, but who would be a poor fit. Create a profile of an individual who might meet all the job specs but would be a disaster long term if you were to hire her. To create this profile, answer the following questions:

- What particular personality trait would rub people the wrong way in your culture? Arrogance? Fickleness? Anger? Laziness? Game playing?
- Think of an employee you hired in the past who was a poor fit; why didn't he work out; what particular things did he do or say that hampered rather than helped achieve your mission?

BEWARE OF THE CLONES

Entrepreneurs like to replicate themselves. This is a natural if unconscious reflex; small businesses are frequently tight-knit communities and colleagues become friends. It's not unusual for entrepreneurs to select people who went to the same schools, grew up in the same neighborhoods, and even enjoy the same hobbies. It feels like hiring someone who is the polar opposite (from a personality standpoint) of the CEO is a mistake.

As you know by this point, I believe in shared mission and values. But I also believe in diversity in every sense of that word. People who share values such as authenticity, integrity, and ambition may have wildly different personalities. Distinguish between a considered and articulated culture versus an unspoken cult of personality. In the absence of a clearly defined culture, organizations may default to hiring people who seem reflections of their leaders and will never challenge their policies and strategies.

This is as opposed to people like Steve and Tom who radiate authenticity, but Steve is authentically proud bordering on arrogant, while Tom is genuinely humble and soft-spoken. They both never put on an act, but their authenticity manifests itself in very different ways. Diverse personalities can create positive friction. Diverse backgrounds can create synergistic perspectives. As long as values are shared and aligned with the company's mission, entrepreneurial enterprises can and should accommodate this diversity.

To guard against the cloning reflex, therefore, here are techniques that might prove useful:

- Make a distinction between what a candidate believes (values) versus how she expresses these values (behaviors).
- Create a list of your own personality traits and compare it with those of a candidate. If, for instance, you list your own characteristics as "good sense of humor, decisive, quick thinking," assess how close a candidate's traits are to your own.
- Assess your team of employees and determine what you're missing in terms of race, gender, and personality type. Be alert for candidates who possess backgrounds, perspectives, or qualities that your team is missing.

WHAT TO DO IF THINGS CHANGE?

This is a common question entrepreneurs ask, and understandably so. After all, entrepreneurial businesses can be volatile. The business can take off in hyper-growth mode or stall. You can find yourself adding or subtracting products and services. Unexpected opportunities can take you in new directions.

Given the probability of change, why take the time to create mission and values for a business at a given moment in time?

Because it doesn't matter what changes. Mission and values are constant. Yes, you may need to hire someone for a position that didn't exist a few years ago—director of analytics, for instance. You may have to hire more employees with global experience as you expand beyond the United States. But even though these new people may have different expertise and experience than your current employees, they should share values and a sense of mission.

Use the roadmap analogy to remind yourself to focus on values and mission and not just on competencies when hiring. The mission is your destination. If your mission is to get to a beautiful vacation spot with sunshine and beaches, your way of getting there won't change much (unless you're the rare company that does a complete pivot—then your destination becomes a snow-covered mountain). You may slow down or speed up on your journey or take some detours, but you're still moving in the same direction guided by the same values.

Remind yourself, too, that problems will arise if you ignore mission and values in the recruiting process. As you're traveling to your destination, you need to agree how you're getting there (car, plane, train, boat) and if you're driving, how often you stop for breaks or if you want to take the scenic or most direct route. Without shared values, these decisions can create acrimony, high turnover, and failure.

With a shared commitment to the same mission and values, something magical happens. When employees are aligned at these deeper levels, they can move far more quickly and effectively. When problems develop, they produce debate and solutions rather than debate and dissension. When people feel connected, they work harder, smarter, and more innovatively. They are all motivated to get to the same destination, to fulfill an ambitious mission. Albert Einstein is known to have said "everything is vibration" and when core values among people unite, they vibrate at a higher frequency and achieve greatness together.

Keep your mission and values in your consciousness, since you'll need them as you begin examining candidates and assessing whether they embody your work beliefs—or if you just think they do.

CHAPTER 6

Seeing Your Perceptions and Their Realities

ppearances can be deceiving. You're not a mind-reader; you have no way of knowing if half the things a candidate tells you in an interview or lists on a resume are true, since some things simply aren't verifiable—such as when a candidate tells you she is willing to work night and day to turn your company into a world-class organization. But if you consider yourself a good judge of character, you may jump to certain conclusions based on the impression a candidate makes.

Most recruiters assess candidates, but you also have to assess your perceptions of these candidates. This means going deeper into assessment than you've gone before: You have to dig down beneath the specs to see what makes a person tick. Remember, every candidate is going to try and impress you; some will make great first impressions. But to figure out if someone will fit into your entrepreneurial culture, you have to see beyond that first impression. Is a candidate hiding something deliberately?

As you begin to recruit for a position—as you assemble a list of candidates and start interviewing—be aware that you're going to make all sorts of subjective judgments based on what you read about and hear from candidates. You assume a candidate is brilliant because she went to Harvard. You assume that another candidate will be responsible and hard-working because he talks enthusiastically about his family and how devoted he is to doing things with his children. You assume a third candidate will not fit in because she has tattoos and seems too willing to take risks.

You may be right about all your assumptions, but you also may be wrong. That's why you need to test your perceptions. Being aware of *your* perceptions and *their* realities is a second step for implementing the new philosophy of highly effective entrepreneurial recruiting (but remember that these four steps are not necessarily in order).

THE PERSON BEHIND THE CANDIDATE

Consciously or not, job candidates aren't always 100 percent honest. After all, they're trying to sell themselves, and some of them don't believe it's in their best interest to communicate their weaknesses or admit that they're unsure or lack knowledge about a topic. They may also be hiding a more deeply ingrained attitude or work style that is antithetical to your own. In other instances, candidates may not be hiding anything intentionally but are unaware of a particular weakness or knowledge deficit.

You can bring these hidden facets out into the open, but you can't do so if you go into an interview winging it. It doesn't matter if you're perceptive about people or if you've hired lots of good employees in the past. While confidence is a good entrepreneurial quality, false confidence is not. It takes a process to discover the truth about people, a process that involves using the masks and blind spots that I discussed in Chapter 2. Now let's look at how these terms fit into the Johari Window:

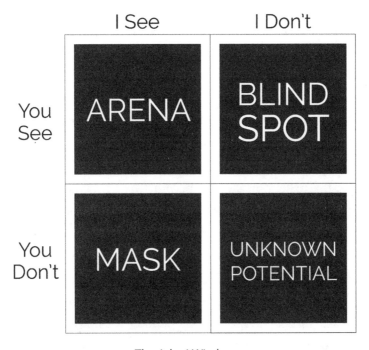

The Johari Window.

On the surface, the Johari Window is deceptively simple. It's designed to assess your perceptions or lack thereof versus a candidate's perceptions or lack thereof. The "You" and the "I" of the Johari Window refers to the entrepreneur (you) and the candidate (I).

In the "You See/I See upper left quadrant, your perceptions and those of the candidate are congruent. For instance, a VP Finance candidate tells you that he's highly skilled at financial duties such as budgeting and tax issues, and his discussion of these issues combined with his resume assure you that what he says is aligned with what you perceive. This quadrant is termed "Arena" because it's the area of a candidate's most significant strength.

In the upper right quadrant—the You See/I Don't See one—your VP Finance candidate claims to be adept at investor relations related to an initial public offering. But you don't see a lot of SEC filings experience in his past and during your conversation he reveals inadvertently his lack of sophisticated knowledge on this subject because his corporate controller handled this set of responsibilities. The candidate isn't trying to deceive you with his VP Finance experience; he is simply overestimating his ability or isn't aware of his knowledge deficit. This quadrant is the "Blind Spot."

The lower left quadrant—I See/You Don't—is one where the candidate is deliberately hiding relevant information—usually information that reflects negatively on him. The VP Finance candidate doesn't tell you that he has had complaints from employees about his unwillingness to help them learn and grow; that rather than spend the time to teach when they make mistakes, he takes on the task and completes it himself. The VP Finance candidate is aware that he is not a good teacher and tends to try and do everything himself, but he also recognizes that this might not help him get the job. If he senses that inspiring followership and mentoring are important to you, he will hide his lack of abilities in this quadrant, the "Mask."

The lower right quadrant—I Don't/You Don't—refers to qualities that don't seem particularly relevant to either of you. For instance, the VP Finance was a member of some social fraternity. Both of you are aware of this fact. On the surface, this isn't a topic of discussion since it has nothing to do with qualifications for the job. But you are impressed that the VP Finance belonged to a social fraternity and you think to yourself, "This guy has potential because he must get along well with others." The problem: This "unknown potential" factor results in candidates being hired or not hired (the other candidate you're considering participated in different extracurricular organizations that actually could have more social skill attributes), when in reality, this factor should have no bearing on a hiring decision. Proven experience and known potential are much better considerations for selecting a hire than unknown potential.

Don't place too much emphasis on the Arena quadrant. You may be impressed by what you see—the experience and expertise of a candidate—and it may jibe perfectly with what the candidate tells you, but this area of perceptual agreement revolves around technical chops, and as I've emphasized in earlier chapters, it's overemphasized by entrepreneurs. Certainly you want someone who is qualified for the job, but too often, emphasizing competence deemphasizes other factors like beliefs and values.

At the same time, don't squander a hire on someone in the lower right quadrant because you see potential based on something the candidate says or has done that has little direct bearing on her qualifications. She may have been a Girl Scout, have received an award from an industry trade group, have great recall of all the customer companies listed on your website, or have served in the Peace Corps, but none of this translates directly into superlative performance within your organization.

The upper right quadrant—Blind Spot—is where you want to find candidates. Most of the time, the future stars enter into your organization with a learning deficit. They don't know everything they should to shine brightly. Don't try to hire a perfect candidate—you'll end up focusing on technical chops to the exclusion of all else. Recognize, too, that all of us are flawed, and you want people to hire individuals whose egos are not so big that they lie to hide their flaws. Instead, look for people who don't realize that they are missing a skill or area of knowledge; who when you discuss this blind spot with them, don't react defensively; who are curious about this area and ask questions and are willing to admit that "I don't know." These candidates usually possess authenticity, humility, and integrity—crucial ingredients for effectiveness in entrepreneurial organizations.

The Mask quadrant is where you'll make your biggest mistakes. During interviews, people who are hiding something come off as supremely confident. They may make a great first impression. Many times, they're excellent self-promoters. What you don't see, however, is that they wear a mask as a survival mechanism and operate from a scarcity mindset. Lacking the confidence to be vulnerable and admit they have areas where they need to grow, they create a false impression of who they are.

Maria ran a small local chain of high-end clothing boutiques, and she wanted to create a website and use social media to grow her revenue beyond her five local retail outlets. As soon as she interviewed Jason, she was convinced she had found someone who would help her achieve this objective. Jason had helped three other small retail companies grow through digital strategies in the last ten years, and two of the heads of these companies provided sterling references, attesting to Jason's great ability in this area. Jason made a convincing case that he thrived when presented with tough challenges, and that he loved taking responsibility for meeting those challenges.

Maria hired Jason, and his skill at helping the company convert their retail offerings to digital was off the charts; he knew what he was doing. The problem: Jason could only work well with people who were like him, who came from a tech background, who were men who had worked in Silicon Valley, and who enjoyed talking about technology. It wasn't that he was hostile to other types of people; it was just that he was indifferent to them. As a result, he created morale problems. People accused him of playing favorites (other geeky tech guys like himself); and he created a site that was technologically superior but didn't represent the brand—it conveyed little understanding of their current and prospective customers. Jason was well aware of his preference to work with like-minded people—it had gotten him in trouble at his previous employer—but he hid it from Maria and in their interview actually claimed that "I can work with anyone."

This is just one example of the danger of masks. As an entrepreneur, be aware that people who are willing to deceive and who hide their weaknesses are walking time bombs. It may be that they have hidden their inability to work well with women; or they are rugged individualists who dislike collaboration; or they are closet bullies who lash out at and blame others when under stress.

And don't rely on references. If you base a hire on sterling references, you're basing it on highly subjective sources. We're in the process of talking to a Harvard MBA for a CMO position at a fast-growing tech company, and our client wants to speak with a COO who worked with the candidate a few years ago. I dissuaded the CEO from doing so, explaining that we don't know the COO's motivation. The COO may have a grudge against the CMO candidate for any number of reasons; or the COO may have been a close friend who is hoping that the CMO will recommend him for a job wherever he lands. Referral sources rarely reveal masks, and that's a critical goal.

In today's workplace, you can't tolerate these masks. Workplaces are increasingly diverse and dependent on collaboration. To introduce someone who is intolerant or arrogant or disingenuous into an inclusive entrepreneurial culture is asking for trouble.

Direct assessment is the best way to identify masks as well as blind spots; let's examine how you can do so.

DIFFERENTIATING BLIND SPOTS FROM MASKS

On the surface, it's simple: You're looking for people who have the capabilities to do the job but don't realize exactly where it is they fall short. You're looking for candidates who aren't defensive about a weakness but are honestly interested in figuring out why and how they are weak and eager to learn and turn that weakness into a strength.

In practice, however, making this determination isn't easy. People are complicated, and blind spots and masks both involve elements that are hidden from view. Differentiating who is hiding something purposefully versus someone who is doing so unknowingly can be challenging.

No matter how perceptive you might be about people—and as I've noted, entrepreneurs are often more astute in this area than most—you shouldn't assume that you can read candidates just by having a casual interview conversation with them. Instead, rely on tactics to help you form pictures of individuals that will give you clues as to whether they possess a blind spot or a mask. Specifically, engage in conversations with candidates about their achievements and accomplishments and monitor their reactions.

It's not just what they say but how they say it. Just about everyone you'll interview for a managerial-level job is proud of something— of orchestrating an acquisition, of implementing a new process or policy, of solving a tricky problem, of building a team. Encourage people to talk about their accomplishments and how they achieved them. Ask questions such as:

- Looking back at your last job and jobs throughout your career, what stands out as the accomplishment which you're most proud of; what do you think was significant about achieving or exceeding a particular objective?

- How much responsibility do you have for achieving this objective; did you do the bulk of the work yourself or did others deserve credit?

- Thinking back to what you achieved, is there anything you might have done differently or better and achieved even greater results?

- How do you feel about this accomplishment; what does it mean to you; beyond achieving a goal or solving a problem, do you have a deeper sense of the significance of this win?

People's responses to these questions generally fall into two broad categories. Some will use the pronoun "I" frequently, take responsibility for most if not all of the achievement, and speak at length about related skills, knowledge, and achievements. In the other category, people will take credit for the achievement but also note the contributions of others. They will also admit that luck and other factors played a role in their success. And they will be open about their concerns early on in a given project, how they were anxious about whether they would succeed or at least uncertain about the outcome.

Pay attention to the candidate's body language, tone of voice, and the entire gestalt of his response. Assess whether he's an arrogant bragger or confident and humble. Is he gesturing aggressively and does he speak pedantically? Or does he possess a calm but purposeful demeanor and a sincere and measured tone of voice?

People with blind spots will readily admit that they don't know something. But they will also demonstrate curiosity as you explore a topic where they may lack knowledge. They'll ask you questions about what they might do to gain knowledge or experience; they will communicate a desire to learn.

People with masks will be defensive if you touch on an area where they have problems or lack knowledge. They won't, however, admit to any type of weakness and instead will rationalize why something isn't important for them to know or dismiss it as irrelevant; or they may even pretend to possess knowledge they lack. Perhaps more disturbingly, they'll be uncomfortable if you start asking them about these areas or about past failures. It's quite possible that they have convinced themselves they don't need to learn and grow and will never fail, that they lack self-awareness. Whatever the reason, they don't possess the agility and learning capacity that entrepreneurial organizations need from their key people.

As you're reading this, you may be thinking to yourself that a candidate with a blind spot may not be that much better than one with a mask. If an individual doesn't realize she isn't good at something or has a particular weakness, won't she be a liability rather than an asset? Entrepreneurs tend to want to get things done now, and they are understandably worried if a candidate lacks a skill or needs more expertise.

If you're thinking in these terms, remind yourself that blind spots are easily remedied. They speak much more to a lack of exposure to an area of work or a lack of corporate maturity. If the candidate demonstrates an eagerness to learn, learning on the job combined with awareness of the gap is more than enough to do the trick.

A mask, on the other hand, can't be remedied through awareness and development. In fact, you need to be especially vigilant for masks because behind them are five types of employees you don't want anywhere near your business.

SCREEN CANDIDATES WITH
FIVE RED FLAGS IN MIND

As you assess people who are applying for a position in your company, you and your selection team will probably encounter scores of seemingly qualified candidates, at least from the standpoint of job specs. You will also encounter a number of candidates who present well, who wear their masks so expertly that you won't see what lurks behind them—at least at first glance.

To help you identify the five dangerous types who come to interviews wearing masks, let's name and describe each and how you can spot them.

Posers/Pretenders

This type is characterized by excessive pride, hubris, and envy. In organizations, these executives never admit they've made mistakes and will cover them up rather than face these errors and fix them. Secretly insecure, they are terrified of being exposed, so they will project false confidence and never admit to doing anything wrong. They envy other people's success and like nothing better than taking people down a peg with snide remarks behind their backs. Perhaps the most devastating consequence of having a Poser/Pretender in your organization is that they allow problems to spiral out of control. If they feel like they might be blamed for something, they will hide or ignore it rather than address it before it gets worse.

In interviews, however, Posers/Pretenders may come across as supremely confident. It may appear as if they rarely make mistakes. Entrepreneurs are especially likely to hire these individuals for leadership positions, since they project traditional leadership qualities—decisiveness, control, confidence. But their mask may slip if you press them on problems that occurred under their watch at previous employers. If they become defensive or scapegoat others, that's a sign that they're hiding something behind their leadership mask.

Political Beasts

As the name implies, Political Beasts are game players and power lovers. They seek the most influential people in an organization, aligning themselves with powerbrokers. They eschew hard work, preferring to manipulate others into doing the work for them. Because entrepreneurs often run smaller companies where good morale and work habits are crucial, Political Beasts can have a devastating effect. Employees may spot a Political Beast long before an owner does, and the Beast's behavior is alienating: Employees wonder about the entrepreneur's judgment and how she could have been so naïve as to hire this individual.

It's not naivete as much as the convincing mask this candidate wears during the recruitment and selection process. In many cases, Political Beasts have gone to the best schools—they have MBAs from top schools, for instance. They also know how to play all types of games, including the interview game. They understand how to curry favor and make a good impression; they have plenty of charm when they want to use it.

During interviews, though, you may be able to spot a Political Beast. People who name-drop are likely to be political animals. While you're talking to them, they "casually" mention that they know a CEO of a big company, a celebrity, a professional athlete. Another telling sign: They express enthusiasm only for high-level tasks like "strategy" and little enthusiasm for rolling up their sleeves and for the less glamorous aspects of managerial life (like developing people). A third sign: They betray an elitist, entitled sensibility. They may articulate this subtly during the recruitment process—dismissing less prestigious jobs and companies, acting as if they deserve the job rather than that they have to make a case for themselves—but if you sense that they act like they're better than others, they may well be Political Beasts.

Troublemakers

These individuals are overly judgmental and blame others when things go wrong. They're the people in a company who exacerbate rather than manage conflict between two of their team members. They like pitting people against each other. They're the ones who will say to you, "We've got to get rid of Mary; she's the one that's causing the team to underperform," even when Mary isn't at fault. They are not team players. Instead, they like to create tension and manufacture problems; they get bored when things are going smoothly.

When you're recruiting a Troublemaker, you may be impressed by their judgments. They have opinions about everyone and every process and policy. They may even articulate these judgments well and make a good case for why a policy is outmoded or why the head of accounting is behind the times. If they have a skill, it's the ability to point out flaws. But the mask they wear is one of competence, when in fact they are only adept at pointing out things that are wrong. They are terrible at managing people and helping achieve consensus. And they're especially inept when it comes to seeing people's strengths and helping them succeed.

Beware the candidate who tells you all the things that are wrong with his former employer or with your company. It may seem as if he's perceptive and analytical, but really, all he wants to do is create turmoil.

Lone Wolves

This type is especially appealing to many entrepreneurs, in that they seem to embody the rugged individualist spirit that classic entrepreneurs possess. While they may be rugged individualists, they are also me-first people who don't listen to others. If you're looking for someone who is inclusive and sees organizations as familial, Lone Wolves are not your people. They romanticize themselves, believing that they and they alone are capable of achieving a goal. They have their own personal agendas, and they'll drive toward them ruthlessly, ignoring the larger organizational mission. Lone Wolves may be able to function effectively in certain positions, as long as they don't have to work closely with others and they're closely supervised.

If you interview a Lone Wolf, she may come across as assertive, and she may try to align her personal agenda with the larger entrepreneurial one. Initially, she may seem perfectly agreeable, but if you push her, you'll discover the anger beneath the surface. Ask suspected Lone Wolves tough questions and push them on their answers. Can they maintain their equanimity? Or do you see them start to seethe? They're going to try and hide that anger from you, but you'll glimpse it if you push. Also, question them about their work styles. Do they like to work in teams? Are they able to relate to a diverse group of customers? Can they provide an example from their past in which they were members of a great team that achieved great things? If they keep bringing their answers back to what "I" accomplished or how they prefer to function autonomously, then you're probably looking at a Lone Wolf.

Wallflowers

These individuals seem like the most benign of all the types, since they are very nice people who no one will say a bad word about. Unfortunately, they're the people who are satisfied to work at 30 percent capacity. They don't engage fully when working on a project and never extend themselves or take on stretch assignments. Many times, Wallflowers are paradoxically engaged and active in their social lives; they may have a hobby that they love and where they are fully engaged. Work, though, is just a means to an end— to a fabulous vacation or early retirement. Even more insidious, Wallflowers bring out the worst in others. They're the ones that convince fellow employees to take longer-than-normal lunch breaks, to waste time watching YouTube videos when they should be working.

The masks Wallflowers wear are composed of affability, tolerance, and open-mindedness. During interviews, you immediately like them and think your people will also like them. They seem made for teams, and even if they don't strike you as dynamos, you assume that they'll become more engaged as they become comfortable working for the company.

Here's a test that will help you identify a Wallflower. During interviews, ask him how he feels about having to work on weekends or describe a project in which your people worked around the clock to meet a deadline. If you see hesitancy on the part of the candidate—he tells you that sometimes he can't work weekends because he helps take care of his elderly mother—then it may be a sign of a Wallflower. Similarly, if he starts rationalizing why it's not necessary to work as hard as you're suggesting ("I've always found I can get my work done twice as fast as most people"), then he may be a Wallflower.

CREATING AND CAPITALIZING ON A SAFE INTERVIEW ENVIRONMENT

Don't turn interviews into inquisitions. If a candidate feels like you're skeptical and suspicious or even that you're relentless and indifferent to her feelings, she probably won't respond honestly. Remember, candidates will deceive you, consciously or not. You need to create an environment where you give them the opportunity to be honest during the interview, where they feel they won't be punished by revealing something about themselves that they perceive to be unflattering. They may not reveal a mask or blind spot explicitly, but they will tell you something that gives you a clue as to whether it's a mask or a blind spot and whether they are humble, authentic individuals or arrogant poseurs.

It would be nice if you just come out and ask, "Are you wearing a mask?" or "Are you being genuine?" But direct questions such as these rarely work. Instead, you need to create an atmosphere in which candidates are encouraged to be honest and open. You can create this atmosphere in the following ways:

- **Focus on having a conversation rather than an interrogation.** Don't keep firing questions at candidates. Encourage them to ask you questions. Don't lock into a formal process or a series of questions that you have to get answered. Instead, create a dialogue that more closely resembles a conversation you'd have with a good friend than a stilted, scripted interview. Be sufficiently relaxed to let the conversation go in whatever direction it may. This will relax the candidate and help him be more willing to disclose his experiences and feelings, closing the gap between what you see versus what he sees.

- **Practice the art of being soft and subtle (and not just hard and provocative).** Think of a lawyer cross-examining a hostile witness—that's the model you don't want to adopt. There can be value in asking tough questions and pushing people to get them to think hard and deeply about a subject, but if this is your default setting, you'll cause most candidates to be defensive or combative and learn little of value. Instead, try to learn about candidates by getting them to tell a few of their stories. Everyone has stories—both about their triumphs and about their failures—and they offer glimpses into blind spots and masks. Ask a candidate to tell you a story about her worst work experience, a time when she faced a career crisis, a situation in which she faced a right-versus-right decision.

- **Don't limit the conversation to work.** People reveal what drives them—their mission and values—not just when they talk about work but when they talk about all aspects of their lives. "What's lighting you up these days?" is a great opener. Do they participate in philanthropic efforts—if so, why? Why did they choose this particular field/career; did they have other aspirations when they were younger? What kind of legacy do they want to leave their children? The next chapter will go into much more detail on mission and values, but here I want to be sure you open up the discussion so that it goes beyond business. In fact, when I first meet prospective candidates, I often postpone business talk for as long as possible and focus instead on the things that interest them, based on my research for a given candidate. This helps build rapport, makes them feel safe and comfortable, and helps us find as much common ground as possible. Shared interests and commonalities bring people together. No one wants a relationship to fail and I make it clear to candidates that I am interested in learning as much as possible about them so I can assist them now and in the future—and relate the discussion to a given position in the present or their future career trajectory. Getting as much information as possible and drawing a complete picture is helpful to recruiters and candidates alike.

If you follow these three suggestions, you'll gain a much greater appreciation for a candidate's hidden weaknesses as well as whether that person is deliberately deceiving you about some aspect of his knowledge or work attitudes and practices. In this environment, you'll also have more freedom to use a technique I've found particularly useful—giving a candidate the opportunity to challenge something you say.

For instance, I'm interviewing a candidate for a sales leadership role where it's absolutely essential to meet or exceed set quotas. During the interview, I might say something like, "I know a lot of companies have strict policies on quotas, but at some companies, if you miss a quota every now and then, it's not a big deal."

What I want is for the candidate to respond that she's never missed a quota, that if you have a lax attitude and miss one, you're likely to miss another, and that it sends a negative signal to salespeople. In the right interview environment, a candidate will feel she has sufficient freedom to voice such an opinion (assuming, of course, that she believes it's not okay to miss quotas). In an inquisition-like environment, however, the candidate will probably just go along with whatever I say, fearing that if she contradicts me, it will rule her out as a candidate.

SEARCHING FOR
HIGH-LEVEL PEOPLE

In the old days, this "high-level" quality was known as character. It referred to someone who possessed strong values, who did the right thing consistently, who was committed and loyal, who was comfortable in his skin. Entrepreneurs have always depended on people with character to help run and manage their companies; they know that in businesses that can be volatile and where risks sometimes must be taken, having individuals who are honest and steady and who work well with others is critical.

Even more now than in the past, entrepreneurs need these high-level people.

Today, we've developed a more sophisticated, psychologically acute understanding of people who possess character. This understanding can guide you as you recruit people for positions of responsibility in your business. As you search for individuals who fall into the upper right quadrant of the matrix and as you attempt to weed out the masked candidates who exhibit any of the five deadly sins, use the following three screens to help find high-level employees:

Maslow's Hierarchy of Needs

Maslow believed that there is a hierarchy of human needs, as pictured on the next page:

The higher up you go on the pyramid, the better you can satisfy your own needs and contribute to teams and the larger business. When you interview people, try and place them on the pyramid.

Maslow's Hierarchy of Needs.

Most candidates will be able to satisfy needs on the first two levels, and a significant percentage will be at the third level. Candidates at the fourth and fifth levels are likely to be terrific employees and managers and leaders as well.

Jim Collins's Level 5 Leadership

If you're interviewing people for a leadership position, pay attention to Jim Collins, author of *Good to Great*. Notice that Collins's Level 5 executive is a "paradoxical blend of personal humility and professional will." If you're interviewing someone and you notice this

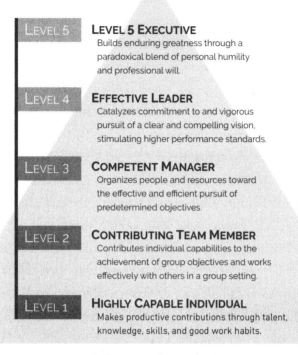

LEVEL 5 — **LEVEL 5 EXECUTIVE**
Builds enduring greatness through a paradoxical blend of personal humility and professional will.

LEVEL 4 — **EFFECTIVE LEADER**
Catalyzes commitment to and vigorous pursuit of a clear and compelling vision, stimulating higher performance standards.

LEVEL 3 — **COMPETENT MANAGER**
Organizes people and resources toward the effective and efficient pursuit of predetermined objectives.

LEVEL 2 — **CONTRIBUTING TEAM MEMBER**
Contributes individual capabilities to the achievement of group objectives and works effectively with others in a group setting.

LEVEL 1 — **HIGHLY CAPABLE INDIVIDUAL**
Makes productive contributions through talent, knowledge, skills, and good work habits.

Jim Collins's Level 5 Leadership.

paradox—someone comes across as self-effacing yet also seems to have an indomitable drive to get things done—then you're probably interviewing a viable candidate.

Growth Mindset

Carol Dweck, a Stanford University psychology professor, discovered "fixed" and "growth" mindsets while studying the behavior of schoolkids in the early 2000s. She found that starting from childhood, people often fall into two outlooks on intelligence: a fixed mindset or a growth mindset. Those with a fixed mindset think that success is based upon fixed traits—they believe that they are either born smart or flawed, and their entire lives are defined by a set amount of intelligence and capability. They are often learning- and risk-averse, preferring tasks that they already do well.

On the other hand, those with a growth mindset know that excellent performance depends upon perseverance, hard work, and learning from failure. For those with a growth mindset, life is ripe with opportunities and there is no failure—only challenges to overcome on the path to mastery.

Therefore, watch for how candidates respond to questions about learning and failure. While no one is going to say, "I hate to learn new things" or "I never take risks," some people will prefer work that's in their sweet spot and not be particularly interested in taking on stretch assignments or tackling projects with high risk of failure. Conversely, some people love to learn, not just at work but in life; they're signing up for courses, trying new hobbies, and reading all sorts of books.

WHAT'S GOING ON
BENEATH THE SURFACE?

As I noted at the start of the chapter, you have to perceive deeper if you want to hire a great employee. Stephen Prothero, a Boston University professor and authority on world religions, has written about how atheists and others ask him why religion is important, and he responds that it's not important what you believe, but that you recognize that most other people have different beliefs than you do. Most critically, he makes the point that if you want to lead and influence others, you need to understand their beliefs.

This means going deeper in your assessment process. Here, I've helped you take the plunge, but now it's time to start evaluating what motivates people at their core, what they believe in fervently, and what they want to accomplish at work and in their lives. In other words, what are their values and what is their mission? What is their "why"?

CHAPTER 7

Drivers

Mapping the Candidates' Missions and Values

The second step of the process—seeing your perceptions and their realities—took you deeper into who candidates are than most recruiting approaches. In this third step, you need to go deeper still so you can figure out what makes a person tick. Fortunately, you've gained insights about individuals that offer clues to their characters. Now, the challenge is to acquire some additional information and then learn to analyze values-based data.

To help you do this, recognize that people possess different drivers or missions. Some are driven by money—they work in order to make a fortune. You can find people like this in all businesses (though they're especially prevalent on Wall Street), and they measure success by the money they make each year or from each deal. Others are driven by a desire to change the world—or at least the sector of the world that their work impacts.

After Mary Lou Song had helped eBay become enormously successful, she was looking for a new challenge. To figure out where she wanted to go next, she created a list of what she really wanted from her work. At the top of her list was this statement: To be surrounded by people with similar values. More specifically, she wanted to work with people who were in high-growth modes and also were eager to take risks and learn from them. Values rather than titles, company fame, or compensation drove Mary. As she jokingly said, "If I had discovered (the right mix of people) at a cupcake bakery, that would have been just fine too."

Mary Lou Song's drivers were risk, learning, and growth, but your candidates may have very different types of drivers. If you hire someone whose driver doesn't fit those of you and your company, that person will fail to live up to your expectations. Let's say you hire the most competent vice president on the planet—she has amazing skills that are exactly what you need for the job. But if she's driven by money and you're driven by making a lasting impact, then she'll always fall short. She'll never see your vision for the company and be willing to sacrifice short-term financial achievement for long-term enterprise building. Or she won't be able to grow and motivate her people because there's no financial incentive to do so. Or she'll perform well for a short period of time but leave as soon as she receives a better offer.

And then there's how people seek to achieve their mission—the values that govern their behaviors. Some people are ruthless and dictatorial. Others are compassionate and generous. These values have a profound effect on other employees; again, you want to make sure a candidate's values synch with your own and those prized by your culture.

To make these assessments, let's consider the range of personal missions and values of candidates and define the most common ones.

BECOME AWARE OF
WHO A CANDIDATE REALLY IS

People are more than the sum of their expertise and experience. You don't really know a candidate—or know if he will fit in your company and help it grow—unless you make the effort to assess his drivers. Why does John work; what does he hope to accomplish in his career; what does he want his legacy to be; how do his values govern his work style? These are just some of the questions that need to be answered, and to obtain these answers, it helps to know the common missions and values that people possess. Let's start with the missions:

Ambition

These individuals want to become CEOs or secure other capstone positions. They are driven by promotions, by climbing whatever ladder exists in a company. Advancement through the ranks is what fuels their fire, and they measure their success by how quickly they advance.

For instance, I hired Alan as a salesperson at HotJobs. He was only twenty-four—but he had it all. He was a great guy and possessed the skills you'd want in an entrepreneurial salesperson: He was smart, quick, affable, and best of all, customers loved him. And he knew how to close a sale. He quickly became a star salesperson at HotJobs, but Alan quit ten months into his tenure, when he was two months away from vesting his first tranche of stock options that at the IPO would have been worth $2.5 million. He quit because he felt like he wasn't getting promoted fast enough.

The moral of the story: If you interview a candidate who is primarily motivated by ambition, make sure you are able to put him on a fast track and keep him there. You should also be sure that your company's culture will accommodate a highly ambitious individual. Ambitious people can be impatient and impetuous, especially when their career trajectory doesn't meet their expectations. Their behaviors can be counter-productive when their need for immediate gratification (i.e., promotions) supersedes their willingness to take the long view. If you have the type of company that can satisfy this need for fast upward mobility, then this individual may perform superlatively. If you don't, then watch out. This rising star can flame out and either quit like Alan did or alienate other employees with his impatience and growing dissatisfaction.

Money

Just about everyone wants to be compensated fairly for their work, but for some employees, this is the be-all and end-all of their existence. Just as some people live for promotions, others live for salary increases, bonuses, stock options, and so on.

At thirty-two, Jerry already had worked for six different companies. A talented engineer, he was especially skilled at creating innovative software programs for the financial services industry. As a result of this skill, he regularly received offers. Whenever an offer was especially good—if it represented a significant bump in salary and other compensation—he would accept it. Jerry didn't weigh other factors before accepting an offer. He didn't care if he liked the people he worked with, how the company was positioned for long-term success, or if he was working on significant projects. His goal was to keep increasing his salary, and though Jerry added a lot of value to his employers because of his skill, his money fixation also limited his contributions. For an entrepreneur seeking an employee who was interested in developing people, contributing to long-term strategic thinking, and facilitating teams, Jerry was not the right candidate. His drive created a kind of myopia, where Jerry could only focus on doing what he did well to justify and increase his compensation.

Helping Others/Family

Some employees work for reasons that go beyond themselves and have to do with their families or others who are close to them or with disadvantaged people—the poor, the disabled, and so on. They want to create a good life for their spouse and kids or for their extended family; or they hope to cure a terrible disease or provide food and water to impoverished societies. Sometimes they have specific, situational goals—they have a special needs child who needs expensive healthcare services—and other times it's a more general desire to provide assistance to people they care about, whether family or people in need throughout the world.

Legacy/Contribution

These people want to leave their mark on the world or at least their particular sector of the world. This is a driving force for many entrepreneurs. They want to leave something behind that is bigger than themselves, that changes the way people do things and that will stand the test of time, or that improves lives. The best employees, even though they aren't owners or leaders, will work equally hard to be part of a process that changes something for the better, taking great pride in their contributions.

Thilo Semmelbauer is a board member for Weight Watchers and Movable Ink, venture partner at Insight Venture Partners, and former COO of Shutterstock and Weight Watchers. He grew revenue to $400 million at Weight Watchers and ran a $1.6 billion P&L. At Shutterstock, Thilo grew revenue from $60 million to $400 million and led the company to an IPO with a $3 billion market cap.

Thilo is driven by his desire to make contributions to industries as diverse as health, digital imagery, and email marketing. He told me, "My father would never let us complain at home, one of the things that we weren't allowed to do was complain. It was always about 'Well, what are you going to do that will turn it around, being a positive force and not a negative force?' . . . I hope to be remembered as somebody who was a positive force in the world."

Excellence

Some employees are motivated to do great jobs because they derive intrinsic satisfaction from superior performance. They relish opportunities to excel, to use their skills to the best of their abilities. These are the people who say, "I can't believe I'm being paid for doing something I love." They don't need financial incentives or threats to work hard and well; they possess an inner drive to do a job as well as they possibly can.

The Ironman Executive Challenge is an entire organization of precisely these kinds of individuals who hold themselves to the highest standards of excellence personally and professionally. Many times, members start their days before 5:00 a.m., performing a rigorous program of endurance, strength, and power training. While professional athletes train fifteen hours per week, an Ironman XC athlete may train for more than twenty hours per week while leading companies, being good parents and spouses, and contributing to good causes. To become a member of the challenge, applicants must already be competitive athletes and accomplished business executives. In addition, the Ironman XC competitors are thought leaders in business, value family, and participate in their communities. In short, they pursue excellence in every aspect of their lives.

Obviously, other drivers exist besides these five. I've known leaders whose mission was fame, for instance. It's different than the contribution/legacy driver we discussed, since these leaders are in it for their egos in the present rather than their contributions in the future; they want accolades and publicity rather than to build something that will make people's lives better. Others have a mission of inclusion/affiliation; they want to be part of something, to be valued members of a team or company. Still others are driven by a desire to prove others wrong: They want to show someone in their lives (a parent, a former boss) that they can succeed at a level that this individual said was impossible.

It's worth noting, too, that people often have a mix of drivers. They want to make money, but their primary goal is excellence, for instance. It's that primary driver that's key. Being aware of a candidate's single most important motivation can tell you a lot about fit, even if other motivations exist. Once you know why someone works, you'll have a sense if she'll be a good match for you and your company or if she will have trouble fitting in or staying long.

PROFESSIONAL VIRTUES

While there's some overlap between mission and values, it's useful to think of them separately. Clearly, someone who is driven to help others values generosity. But values also provide another lens for evaluating candidates and whether they will fit with your company.

They speak more to the inherent beliefs and corresponding behaviors of an individual rather than her motivation.

Therefore, investigate what I refer to as candidates' professional virtues: personal values translated into a work environment. For instance, one candidate may value hard work while another values his image; one candidate may value compassion while another believes in winning at all costs. Like missions, values can range far and wide, and my purpose here isn't to list all possible values or even to make judgments on what is a good versus a bad value. Instead, let's focus on six key professional virtues and how they manifest themselves in work environments. If candidates possess one or more of these virtues—and they resonate with the values you espouse in your company—then the odds are good that they'll become high performers if you hire them.

The six virtues are:

Humility

No doubt, you have friends and family members who you would characterize as humble. They rarely brag about their accomplishments. When they do something significant, they prefer to talk about how they couldn't have done it without help, luck, or some other external factor. While they may be proud of what they've accomplished as a parent, a sibling, or in a philanthropic effort, they talk a lot more about their kids or favored causes rather than themselves.

In work situations, this virtue is of inestimable worth, since people love to work with those who are humble. They are great team members since they don't try to dominate the team. They are great team leaders because they foster inclusion (rather than the exclusion practiced by egocentric team leaders).

They may have blind spots, but they're sufficiently humble that they're willing to learn and train and grow in order to address this weakness.

Here are some telling actions of individuals who value humility:

- Eagerness to give fellow employees/direct reports credit when they receive praise
- Discomfort when they feel they are receiving too much credit
- Desire to help others succeed at tasks and in their work roles
- Propensity to refer to we (or us) rather than me (or I)
- Joy and enthusiasm when talking about collaborative success; a more muted tone when discussing individual success

Authenticity

Employees who are genuine—who don't put on a work mask and try to be something they're not—are usually excellent communicators, strong managers, and productive workers. They don't play games or have secret agendas. Instead, they are straight talkers, and people believe them when they say something. In a small, entrepreneurial business they can fit in quickly. Even new hires in top positions are accepted quickly if they exhibit authenticity.

To a certain extent, you identify authentic people instinctively. You know if someone is trying to act like she knows more than she does or when she's putting on airs. You can spot certain types of phonies quickly in interviews, since you can tell they're bad actors. Other times, though, it's difficult to know based on one or two exposures in interviews. Therefore, keep the following traits of professional authenticity in mind:

- Says what's on their mind about a past work situation, even if it's negative or might offend
- Admits flaws in terms of experience or expertise
- Deals directly with tough questions; won't change the subject or offer vague answers
- Allows idiosyncratic or eccentric qualities to emerge in interviews (i.e., a sarcastic sense of humor or a passionate interest in a work subject); doesn't play it cool or try to be an emotionless professional

Compassion/Generosity of Spirit

Some people are great to work with because they bend over backward to help others. They are willing to share their knowledge and when they see someone struggling, they make an effort to assist. They don't hoard what they know because they believe it will give them a competitive advantage from a career standpoint. Instead, they enjoy teaching others without any expectation of reward for their efforts. In entrepreneurial companies that depend on informal exchanges of knowledge (unlike big corporations with formal training programs), this trait is valuable, and generous leaders and managers can make a huge difference in how quickly employees get up to speed.

Here are some identifying characteristics of this value in work settings:

- Shares knowledge about the industry readily and without reservation
- Talks proudly about those they've mentored
- Responds positively to questions about willingness to spend time developing others

- Expresses interest in company programs designed to contribute to the community or other groups in need; wants to participate in these pro bono/philanthropic endeavors

Openness/Transparency

Some companies have closed door cultures; managers are always shutting others out literally or figuratively. Typically, these companies are run by entrepreneurs who are paranoid about competitors getting wind of a new product or worried that their people or concepts will be filched. As a result, employees walk around with a looking-over-their-shoulder mentality and are guarded in their digital and verbal communications.

People who value openness, though, aren't overly concerned with what others know or do. They're much more focused on a free exchange of information and ideas, and they are both open to suggestions from a diverse range of employees and willing to share their own thoughts. They also make themselves vulnerable. They are willing to express ideas that they know may be wrongheaded. They value brainstorming and trying out a variety of concepts. They are willing to take the risk that others might criticize them later.

Candidates who value openness exhibit the following behaviors:

- Take risks in their business projections and theories, talking about projects in ways that suggest they're not worried about being wrong or taking flak if time proves them wrong
- Discuss their fears and problems rather than just their hopes and solutions; they admit when they're anxious about an event, project, or their own capacities

- Request input from others. They are open to outside opinions and are proactive in seeking them

Positive Attitude

Most entrepreneurs I've worked with possess a positive outlook. Optimism is a choice. If they weren't optimistic, they probably wouldn't be able to take the risks that come with the territory. To sustain a positivist culture, however, you need to hire positive people. Negativity spreads fast, especially during downturns, and filling the managerial ranks with optimistic, can-do people helps insulate companies from this negativity.

Don't mistake positivity for a Pollyanna mindset. The latter is unrealistic and can get a company in trouble; you don't want employees in positions of responsibility who fail to see warning signs. Being positive simply means approaching decisions, people, and other situations with pragmatic optimism. If these situations warrant negative actions—firing a poor performer, pulling out of a deal, giving customers bad news—then they must be taken. But employees who look first for possibilities and solutions (rather than becoming obsessed with negative outcomes) are the ones who move entrepreneurial companies forward.

Here are some traits to watch for when interviewing candidates:

- Focuses conversation on present and future rather than the past
- Acknowledges negative events but frames them as things to rebound from rather than become mired in
- Relishes sketching best-case scenarios and specific actions that can make them happen

- Addresses company problems from a potential solution perspective

Hard Work

Again, this is a value near and dear to most entrepreneurs' hearts. But not everyone you'll interview embraces this value. Sometimes, even the most skilled and experienced candidates don't like to put in the hours most entrepreneurial businesses demand of them. In fact, some feel their talent entitles them to a pass from long hours.

Of course, everyone is going to present themselves as possessing this value; it's difficult to imagine someone being interviewed for a job saying, "I'm not into working weekends or past five." So it may not be readily apparent if a candidate truly values hard work. Still, you may be able to tell if working diligently is valued by watching for these traits:

- Tells you a story about a project or accomplishment of which they're proud and mentions the amount of time and effort it required
- Demonstrates stamina—talks about doing something where others quit but they persisted (might not be work-related but involve running a marathon, volunteering for a political candidate)
- Expresses willingness to do whatever it takes to achieve objectives; does not express reservations about the time or effort required for these objectives

When considering these values, be aware that it's unlikely to find all six in any given individual. More likely, you'll discover that a candidate values one or two of them above the others. When you make this discovery, ask yourself: Does this candidate's main value resonate with my own and that of this company's culture?

To answer this question, you need to look deeper into candidates than you have in the past. Let's look at what "deep" means and how you can see beneath candidates' surfaces.

PROBING THE DEPTHS

What every entrepreneur wants to know before making a hire is: What am I not seeing about this candidate? Differentiating between the external perception candidates are capable of creating and their internal truths is the challenge.

To meet this challenge, look at the following graphic of the Iceberg/Honne Model and consider the numbers on the "iceberg" and what they might represent to you:

1. Technical chops—individual contributor, mastery of a craft
2. Ability to collaborate and amplify team spirit toward the achievement of the mission
3. Organization and planning of not only the work but the people around achievement of a stated mission
4. Inspiring followership—being able to inspire, to paint a picture of how the achievement of the team's mission is tied to personal excellence
5. Humility/determination—high degree of personal excellence and desire for achievement as well as the humility required to lead a high-performance team and the agility to pivot

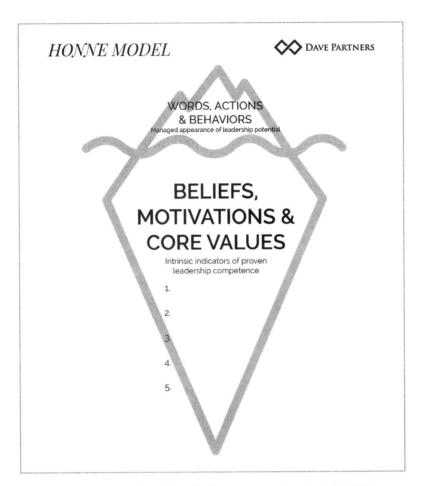

HONNE MODEL

DAVE PARTNERS

WORDS, ACTIONS
& BEHAVIORS
Managed appearance of leadership potential

BELIEFS,
MOTIVATIONS &
CORE VALUES
Intrinsic indicators of proven
leadership competence

1.

2.

3.

4.

5.

Go to www.HireSmartFromTheStart.com to download this PDF
and other resources.

The odds are that you'll be able to figure out the answer to number 1 without digging too deeply in your interviews. But as the numbers get higher, the degree of difficulty of finding the answers becomes greater. If you confine yourself to the standard interview questions—What was the most critical skill you learned at your last job? What are your goals as a leader and how do you think this job can help you achieve them?—then you're not going to go very deep into who the candidate is.

To bring out candidates' mission and values, you need to ask questions that may make candidates a bit uncomfortable—and that may be out of your comfort zone as well. But the discomfort is worth it if you can find someone who will contribute to your company on a high level for years to come.

To dive deeper, consider asking candidates the following questions around the four lower levels of the iceberg:

- How well do you get along with other people? Have you ever had conflicts on teams in which you've been a member or leader—conflicts that hurt the team's effectiveness? Can you give me an example of how you helped a team become more cohesive and work together to reach a stretch goal?

- Do you relate well to a diverse group of people? As a middle-aged white male, can you work productively with women, Millennials, people of color? What is the worst thing that a colleague or direct report has ever said to you; was there any truth in what they said?

- How do you inspire the people with whom you work? What do you say or do that creates excitement around and involvement in the completion of a project? Can you describe a situation where something you said or did inspired others to work to their full potential?

- Does it kill you not to achieve something you set out to do? Are you so determined to meet a deadline, a quota, or other objective that you are almost obsessive in your focus? If we were to survey the people who know you best, would they say that you don't take enough credit for your accomplishments?

Feel free to ad lib based on these questions. Use them to start conversations that probe candidates' depths, encouraging them to reveal aspects of themselves that they might not ordinarily discuss in a job interview.

In addition, you can access other tools for digging deeper in interviews. When presented correctly (with signed authorization from a candidate in advance), you can draw from a variety of behavioral and personality assessment instruments (and I suggest seeking the advice of an employment attorney before implementing for interviewing purposes). Here is a short list of tools that are worth exploring:

DISC Personality Test

DISC is a behavior assessment tool based on the DISC theory of psychologist William Moulton Marston, which centers on four different behavioral traits: dominance, influence, support, and caution.

Myers-Briggs Type Indicator® (MBTI®)
Personality Inventory

The purpose of the Myers-Briggs Type Indicator® (MBTI®) personality inventory is to make the theory of psychological types described by Carl Jung understandable and useful in people's lives.

Hogan Personality Inventory

The Hogan Personality Inventory (HPI) describes normal, or brightside personality—qualities that describe how we relate to others when we are at our best. Whether your goal is to find the right hire or develop stronger leaders, assessing normal personality gives you valuable insight into how people work, how they lead, and how successful they will be.

Watson-Glaser Critical Thinking Appraisal

Watson-Glaser™ Critical Thinking Appraisal was developed in 1925 to assess critical thinking ability and decision making.

TTI

For over thirty years, TTI Success Insights has researched and applied social and brain science, creating behavioral assessments used to hire, develop, and retain talent.

How the World Sees You Assessment

Branding expert Sally Hogshead developed the How to Fascinate program and the How the World Sees You personality test. The assessment helps you discover the exact words to sell yourself to prospects, the types of tasks that fit your personal brand, and which of the forty-two personality archetypes show you at your best.

Kolbe Assessments

Backed by more than thirty years of research and practical applications, Kolbe Assessments provide a map of an individual's natural instincts, or modus operandi (MO).

Herrmann Brain Dominance Instrument

The Herrmann Brain Dominance Instrument (HBDI) measures and describes thinking preferences in people. It was developed by William "Ned" Herrmann while he led management education at General Electric.

Belbin

Over a period of more than nine years, Meredith Belbin and his team of researchers based at Henley Management College, England, studied the behavior of managers from all over the world. Managers taking part in the study were given a battery of psychometric tests and put into teams of varying composition, in which they engaged in a complex management exercise. Their different core personality traits, intellectual styles, and behaviors were assessed during the exercise. During his research, Meredith found that each of the behaviors was essential in getting the team successfully from start to finish. The key was balance.

Wonderlic

Wonderlic provides businesses and schools with a comprehensive library of highly regarded assessments and surveys for each phase of the hiring and student selection process. The Wonderlic test has been a staple of the NFL Draft Combine for years and has a long history as one of the first short-form tests for cognitive ability. In its 75-year history, Wonderlic has delivered over 200 million assessments and surveys for more than 75,000 organizations, government agencies, and accrediting bodies.

CHAPTER 8

Extract
the Matches

Y
ou've found the candidate you want to hire. He possesses the skills and experience that ensure he'll be able to do the job with a high level of competency today, and that he will still be well-qualified as the job's requirements evolve over time. More than that, you believe he'll be a great fit. His personality, beliefs, work style, and long-term goals all dovetail with your company and its culture. You know that he'll help you achieve your company's objectives and that you'll help him fulfill his objectives.

Candidates like this one are usually in high demand. You're not the only one who recognizes his technical chops. You're not the only one who feels he would make an ideal employee. As a result, this candidate probably already has a good job. He may also have offers from one or more of your competitors. And one of the offers may be from a global corporation with an incredible marketplace reputation, while you're a much smaller entrepreneur known only in a relatively limited space.

To get him to say yes, then, may seem like a huge challenge. However, if you've done your recruiting due diligence—assessed your perceptions and the candidate's realities, mapped his missions and values as well as your own—then you have a good chance of convincing a candidate to accept your offer. To take advantage of this knowledge you've gained, the next step is learning how to make an offer he can't refuse—or at least one to which he has to give serious consideration.

ASSESS THE LEVEL OF YOUR OFFER

Entrepreneurs who make job offers at the lowest level usually fail to get their candidates. To understand "lowest," think about Maslow's Hierarchy of Needs and how at the very bottom of his hierarchy pyramid are the things people need to survive—food, water, shelter, and so on. When you try to lure a candidate primarily with a high salary, then you're making a low-level offer. The right candidate—the one who fits the best with your mission and values—probably won't accept the money-focused offer, since he wants a lot more from a job than financial compensation. Even if he does accept it, you've hired a mercenary rather than a missionary. Odds are, this individual will leave sooner rather than later when he receives a better offer.

To avoid making this mistake, consider five stages of offers and determine where yours falls:

- **Stage I—Money.** You offer a great salary and other perks—bonuses, equity in the company, etc. You believe you can't get the candidate to accept the offer unless you sweeten it with cash. The essence of your offer is: "We'll pay you more than anyone else."

- **Stage II—Ego.** You make an offer that is designed to flatter, to make the candidate feel that she will be treated like royalty. You offer an impressive-sounding job title; a luxurious office; a larger staff than the candidate has ever had before; a guarantee of first-class travel and accommodations for business trips. You also make a pitch that she will have a chance to be a superstar in the new position, to be recognized as a trailblazer in the industry and not just within the company.

- **Stage III—Freedom.** You offer the chance to operate with greater independence than the candidate has ever had. Perhaps you tell him that he will have complete decision-making authority over an area; or that he doesn't have to report to anyone except you; or that he has total authority to handpick his team. In other words, you give him the opportunity to run a function, business, or team exactly as he has always dreamed of doing.

- **Stage IV—Impact.** You pitch how your company is going to be the next big thing, and how if she comes on board, she'll be able to make a real difference in your field; that she can change the way your company operates, the nature of a given product or service, and so on. The core of your offer is that this is a place where she can have an effect that is external and not just internal—that it's a job that can make waves in the larger business world. As Stanford University's Irving Grousbeck puts it, recruiting has to have an emotional component. In Grousbeck's words, it might sound something like, "Come work with us, we're doing interesting stuff, we're going somewhere, there's a culture of respect here, we try to work hard and be nice to each other, it's an open learning environment . . . there's some excitement that we're generating here. We may be making washers, but we're making *great* washers, and we plan to expand and do other things."

- **Stage V—Self-Actualization.** You might not use this psychology-based term, but what you're offering is a chance for the candidate to be his greatest self. Most people are driven by this need. They want to rise to their full potential. People are on a quest to achieve this potential, and your offer revolves around the chance to undertake this quest.

There's nothing wrong with making a good monetary offer—people will expect a certain salary base and you need to meet those expectations. But many technically strong candidates will be willing to take less than the best possible offer if you can meet needs at higher levels. Similarly, you can structure an offer to appeal to a candidate's ego, desire for job freedom, and wish to make an impact, and these factors can make your offer more appealing. But if you can link the offer to self-actualization, then you've made the most powerful argument possible.

Our client, Richmond Global was looking to hire a top data science leader. Richmond, headed by Peter Kellner, was a growth stage venture capital firm focusing their investments in the same space occupied by Al Gore's Generation Fund—environment, social, and government. Peter's strategy differed from Gore's in that he leveraged data science to create a successful hedge fund. Data science is a hot area and Standard & Poor's is known to be a leading ratings organization and producer of some of the best data science talent available; experts do well there and are highly skilled. As a result, they are highly valued by their employer and are also courted by the top names in both tech and finance including Google, Facebook, Amazon, BlackRock, KKR, and several others.

Peter needed a data scientist with the right technical chops to head up his firm's efforts in this area. Not only did we need to find someone whose values fit the culture like a glove, but we were competing against much bigger companies who also recruited in this space. During discussions with candidates, I attempted to ascertain who they were—what drove them, what they hoped to accomplish in life. I discovered that one candidate stood out. She had young children to whom she was devoted and relished building communities. She thought a lot about the future and legacy her children would inherit. As we talked, I saw that her personal mission revolved around doing good in the world, and social issues were near and dear to her heart.

Based on this knowledge, Peter and I talked to her about what Richmond hoped to accomplish, and how she could use her data science abilities to help Richmond invest in companies during the early stages (when they really need help) and how this would make the world a better place. The mission and values resonated so strongly that she started crying during the discussion—the tears reflected her joy at having found a job that resonated with her inner drive. As a result of our Stage V offer, not only did we secure a strong hire for Richmond, but it happened only fifty-one days after the search kickoff.

EXTRACTION TACTICS

You may be a great salesperson, but to sell an in-demand candidate on your company, you have to alter your traditional recruiting pitch. Most entrepreneurs talk about how they're offering candidates a great opportunity; how the company is going to grow like crazy and they'll have a chance to be part of a huge success; how the company is like a family and they'll become a member; how they will be given a great office and will have a wonderful staff to support them.

All of this is fine, but it probably isn't sufficient to convince most candidates to leave a great job or to choose your offer over one from a competitor who can pay a higher salary or whose company is better known in the industry or is simply bigger than yours.

In addition, entrepreneurs are often fond of selling candidates on the role they'll play in their companies: "Jack, I've got an opening for a carpenter, and I've got some terrific jobs coming up that I know will challenge you and draw on your skills."

Again, there's nothing wrong with this approach, except that it probably won't work. What might work, however, is if you say to Jack, "I'm building a beautiful palace that will house great works of art. We'll work side-by-side with a brilliant architect and tradesman who are the best in their fields constructing a structure that will be talked about for generations. You're a carpenter; do you want to build the palace with me?"

This approach is all about mission and values, and while it's not guaranteed to convince a candidate to say yes, it stands a much better chance of doing so than other approaches. To use this mission-and-values approach to extract candidates from good jobs (or to win the competition for their services), try the following techniques:

Get Personal

If you confine the discussion to the job, the company, and the industry, then you're not addressing the deeper issues that might trigger a yes to your offer. Therefore, try and encourage candidates to talk about who they are and what they want to become. In addition, create an atmosphere where candidates can relax and talk about themselves. Here's a simple technique: Say the person's name. This is the safest, most reassuring sound they can hear. Look candidates in the eyes with warmth and offer them a genuine smile. Say their name clearly and with energy, accompanied by a firm handshake. Share some of your own story so that others are willing to reciprocate. Share what is most exciting to you presently and explain what drives you longer term, what you hope to achieve in your life and career, how you hope to learn and grow.

One of my favorite questions to get people talking is some variation on: "What are you most excited about?" The more open and safe an environment you create, the more they will be willing to tell you what creates this excitement in their lives. When I volunteer personal information, people tend to want to reciprocate and share more about themselves. Dig a little by asking probing (but not intrusive) questions. For instance, I've found the following question often gets people talking about personal dreams:

Where are you in your life today, and how do you see yourself five years from now?

Encourage them to talk more about the things they disclose without your direct prompting. Legally, some topics are best to stay clear of, like politics, religion, and marital status, so be sure not to probe in these areas. Nonetheless, I might share some of my growth as a parent or struggles with siblings if I sense that this is a topic in their own lives that they'd like to discuss. Remember, people are experts on themselves, and the more you can get them to volunteer about themselves in a safe and comfortable environment, the more you can know them. Most people are especially willing to talk about their children. If they start talking about their sons and daughters, then feel free to follow up with questions or your own observations—if they steer a discussion in this direction, take advantage of their inherent interest in talking about these issues. What kind of future do they hope their children will have? What are their fears for their kids? How do they want their children to see them, what type of legacy do they want to leave, what type of values do they want to impart?

People have all sorts of personal motivations for working. Some love being affiliated with a group of like-valued employees. Some relish the opportunity to innovate and create something better for their customers. Some want power and influence. Some are driven to change the world, to build a company, or to solve a problem that will shift paradigms.

Most candidates won't simply reveal this information in interviews. They may believe that they have to be professional, which means focusing their conversation on job matters. So you have to draw them out, eliciting enough information about what really matters in their lives so that you can demonstrate how taking the job will help them find what they're seeking.

Listen Deeply

This might seem obvious, but you're aiming for a deeper level of listening. If you ask Aditi Javeri Gokhale, Northwestern Mutual's first-ever CMO, for key leadership qualities, one of the first things she'll mention is *empathy* as a way to listen to what people are really communicating—and as a way to motivate and inspire based on what's heard. By listening with feeling, Gokhale describes a process in which leaders listen for the cues that tell them what drives the people around them. What animates them? What really turns them on? Maybe it's career advancement; maybe it's social change. Whatever it is, if you're not listening deeply, you'll miss it, and all your inspirational talk about the company may not carry the candidate along. Listen with feeling and you may discover a driver beneath the surface, something that can help you convince the candidate that your company is where she belongs.

Disrupt Their Thinking

If your preferred candidate is a high-performing professional, odds are that these three basic truths apply: He's good at what he does, people like him, and he's capable of creating circumstances in his life that makes him happy. So he's in a good place, and he may not want to leave that good place unless you disrupt his thinking.

Jar candidates out of their complacency by reminding them of their hopes and dreams—hopes and dreams that they may have pushed to the side. People settle for good enough—for nice salaries, pleasant working conditions, profitable companies. But deep down, they aspire to more. Ask them what they dreamed about becoming when they embarked on their careers. Pose hypothetical scenarios—if they had complete control over a division or company, what would they do? Talk about how we all have a wish for greatness hidden inside of us. Tell them what your wish is and then probe what theirs might be. Don't limit the discussion to work. Maybe their secret wish is to run for elective office or create shelters for the homeless. Talk about this wish and how work might allow them to satisfy it in another way.

Another disruptive technique: Project the future. No one has a crystal ball, but you are probably knowledgeable about your industry and the direction that it's heading. Use this knowledge to forecast changes that may affect candidates' thinking about what is the best job given their aspirations. For instance, about ten years ago Allison was a young but award-winning feature writer for a major market daily newspaper. Allison loved her job and her newspaper, but she was intrigued when a headhunter contacted her about a position at a startup website that needed a writer with strong feature-writing skills to generate high-quality content. Allison interviewed with Hans, the entrepreneur who had started the site, and he told her about how he intended to hire the best young writers from around the world to work for the site and envisioned giving these writers far more freedom to write what they wanted and in the way they wanted than any newspaper would.

Allison was impressed by Hans and his vision for the site, but she was still reluctant to leave what had always seemed to be her dream job. But Hans started talking about the demise of newspapers. He made a compelling case that young people were increasingly going online to find news rather than reading newspapers; that online venues provided writers with opportunities to write longer pieces, to be more creative in their writing, and to develop a following among a young and growing audience. Hans predicted that Allison's newspaper would be in financial trouble within five years and showed her his projections of their declining revenues based on falling circulation and loss of classified advertising monies.

As you might expect, Hans disrupted Allison's thinking, and she eventually agreed to accept his offer.

Create Certainty

The candidate sitting in your office—the one you want to hire—is probably uncertain about everything at this moment. If she has multiple job options, she doesn't know which one to pursue. She may like what you've told her about the position, but she has many questions and doubts. You may have shared your strategy for the company, but she wonders if in five years, it will even vaguely resemble your description. You've disrupted her thinking to the point that her mind is awhirl with possibilities.

If you can create certainty about the future—and candidates see how the picture you paint fits their mission and values—then you may get them to say yes to your offer. How do you create certainty? By doing the following:

- **Be specific.** Provide detail about how you expect the company to evolve, the type of people you will bring into your company, the customers you'll attract, the innovations you'll make.

- **Be passionate.** Speak from the heart. Candidates will be more likely to trust your vision of the future if you display your enthusiasm for and belief in what you're describing. If you're low-key and emotionally neutral, you may seem to have doubts.

- **Be honest and realistic.** As tempted as you may be to use hyperbole, don't. If you project record-setting growth or envision quantum leaps in profits, you'd better be able to justify these numbers or candidates will be dubious. Honesty is a great way to create certainty. People can hear the sincerity in your words and in your tone of voice.

Connect the Dots

This is the clincher. You've teased out their hopes and dreams, their values, their personal mission. You've also painted a picture of where your company will be five years down the road. Now connect their personal mission with your organizational one. How will joining your company help them realize their dreams?

More specifically:

- What opportunities will your company be able to provide a candidate in the coming years in terms of learning, stretch assignments, new skills?

- What potential impact will a candidate be able to make by joining your company, now and in the future? Will he be able to create new programs or design new systems? Will he be allowed to take risks and innovate? Will he have the chance down the line to change the way people think or do things? Will he be able to make a difference in the lives of underprivileged people?

- How are these opportunities and impacts likely to help a candidate fulfill her personal mission?

- Leaders with a large appetite for learning and making a contribution value continued growth opportunities—they know these opportunities will require them to acquire new knowledge and skills and give them platforms for making more significant contributions. They can be among your greatest hires, ever. Remember that the learning and growth that you can offer is attractive to them. The "Four Stages of Competence" model helps identify opportunities for growth and mastery.

PAINTING A PICTURE OF THE FUTURE

As you read about "connect the dots," you may have thought to yourself, "This sounds good in theory, but how do I make this work in practice?" Admittedly, it's a challenge to describe how candidates can achieve their personal mission by describing how the company will evolve in three to five years. But you can meet this challenge if you help candidates visualize that future.

By visualize, I mean using words as well as pictures to help people understand what they might accomplish over time if they join the company. This isn't about making a stump speech full of grand generalities about the company's great resources and strategic

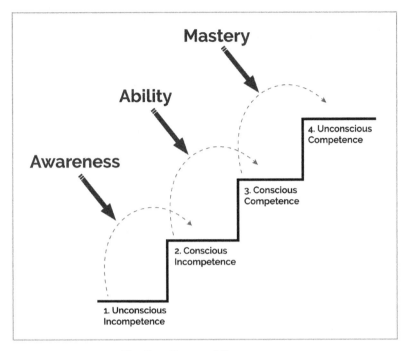

The Four Stages of Competence.

competitive edge. Instead, it requires that you understand candidates' deepest drivers and bring their future at the company to life, helping them grasp in an almost visceral way how the company can satisfy these drivers.

Shutterstock is a New York City–based company that provides a library of photographs, music, and video as well as editing tools that users can license. They were another company looking for someone to head their data science group (data science experts are hot commodities in the tech world), and working with them, we found Shane, who had a terrific job on the West Coast. Not only that, but Shane had a family: His wife had a good job and they loved their California home, climate, neighbors, and schools.

But Shane was the right person for the position, both from technical chops and values standpoints. We needed to find a data scientist who was highly skilled in the personalization of data and he had led teams at both Netflix and Microsoft's Bing program. Shane would be the lead to create a recommendations engine, such as Amazon uses (creating algorithms based on your purchase of books, they recommend other books you might like). We took a look at the twenty-five leading companies in this area and found at least one potential candidate at each company. We then winnowed the list based on interviews designed to identify values.

Shane was head and shoulders above the rest, both from a skills perspective and in terms of how his beliefs and working style fit with the Shutterstock culture. But I knew it would be a challenging sell. As much as I believed that Shutterstock would be as good for Shane as Shane would be for the company, I had to make a compelling argument—an argument that would motivate Shane to sell his family on the move.

Shutterstock's CEO and I created a compelling verbal picture of the company's growth over the next five years and how Shane would be able to fulfill a number of his goals by taking on the position. But what clinched the deal was a video. Shane had talked to me about his personal journey, how he was looking for a company that would allow him to feel a sense of purpose related to his work. His current job was great, but he found that his data science skills were used primarily to create a better customer experience but not an experience that resonated with him personally. He wanted to do something more than build a better mousetrap—or a better algorithm.

When he said that, I knew that Shutterstock would need to show him the video. And so, they did. It was a video of a woman in India. Dressed in colorful silks with a baby resting on her shoulder, she described her experience with Shutterstock tearfully. She talked about how for the first time in her life, she could do something that she was passionate about as well as make enough money to feed her family and send her children to school. She explained that she took photos of India's beautiful landscapes and put them on Shutterstock, and the company had helped her create a market for her images.

During the course of the video, Shane barely moved. He was transfixed not only by the woman's story but by how he could contribute to a company that helped people such as this woman. Shortly thereafter, Shane accepted the offer.

SOMETIMES IT TAKES A VILLAGE . . . OR FOUR GOOD PEOPLE

You don't have to extract a candidate all by yourself. If possible, it's wise to involve others in the recruiting process—both in the interviewing and in the selection/extraction. I've found the best number of people is four—yourself and three colleagues (this can include an outside person—I'm often part of this group). In most instances, the company's CEO is best able to orchestrate the extraction tactics. Because companies are often manifestations of their entrepreneur founders, these CEOs are likely to have the most knowledge and credibility in a candidate's eyes. When they talk about the future and a candidate's place in it, they are often more believable than anyone else associated with the company.

Nonetheless, sometimes a committee can increase the odds of securing a candidate. Here's how:

- **A particular member of your team may connect with the candidate.** During the interviewing period, you may discover that one of your colleagues has established rapport with the candidate. In that case, she may be in a better spot to paint a picture of the future and to help the candidate visualize it.

- **A team member is a great salesperson.** You may have a colleague or consultant who can articulate your company's vision eloquently, who can speak authoritatively and convincingly about the values you prize. This person may also be able to connect the dots in ways that no one else can, helping candidates recognize how they might fulfill their personal mission if they were to accept the offer.

- **Multiple voices carry more weight.** Sometimes, a candidate needs to hear the same message from more than one person. You may do a great job of describing where the company is heading and how a candidate would find his true calling by accepting the offer, but it's only when a second or a third person delivers the same message (in their own words, with their own style) that the message hits home.

- **A collaborative process yields greater insight.** As an individual, you may not see the best way to get a candidate to say yes. As a team, you can discuss this issue and figure out an extraction strategy. You may determine that sharing a white paper written by the founder will open the candidate's eyes to how she fits in the company. A member of your team may suggest showing the candidate video of a philanthropic effort the company participates in. There is no one, ideal tactic to extract a candidate, and brainstorming helps you tailor your approach to suit the candidate.

CHAPTER 9

High-Level Hires

Leaders and Managers

I
n one sense, the process of finding, recruiting, and hiring leaders and managers is no different from the process required to bring in other employees. As always, the skills/competencies component is essential, but not as important as the mission/values element. If you're looking for someone who will fit within your entrepreneurial culture—looking for an individual who will contribute greatly to the company's success now and in the long term—then the key is finding someone whose work style and personal mission and values resonates with your own.

If you're seeking to fill a top leadership or managerial position, however, you've set the bar higher. Whether you're looking for a COO or the head of a function or a key manager, creating clarity around the person and the position is essential. Generalities kill at leadership levels. It will likely result in a poor fit that entrepreneurs especially can ill afford.

Entrepreneurs often run relatively small operations. The number of leadership and senior management positions is limited. As a result, every hire at this level counts. Stanford's Irving Grousbeck quotes the legendary Jim Collins (author of *Good to Great*), referencing the need to "get the A players on the bus in the key seats. No matter what a great leader you may be, if you've got B players in key seats, it's going to be tough slogging."

Making a mistake in recruiting a leader at best will hamper the company's growth and at worst can be fatal. Therefore, I'd like to provide some advice to increase the odds of your finding the right person, as well as to share some stories that will motivate you to be especially diligent when hiring someone for a crucial, high-level position.

A CAUTIONARY
AND AN INSPIRING TALE

Joe was an ambitious entrepreneur. He worked hard and was an expert in the advertising technology industry, having been a valuable individual contributor and manager for the leading companies in this sector. Because of his reputation and contacts, Joe had little difficulty raising venture capital when he launched his startup. Like many neophyte entrepreneurs, Joe was obsessed with controlling expenses. While managing money is essential, especially in the early phases of a company's existence, it can prove problematic when taken to extremes.

Joe figured that he didn't have to spend a lot of money to hire top people for marketing, finance, and legal positions: He felt he knew enough about each area to get by with a small staff of friends and family—people who were loyal to Joe but weren't leaders or managers. More to the point, their values and personal mission had little to do with what Joe believed in. He was driven to pursue growth, and was willing to work to turn his startup into the biggest and best company in its field

After an initial growth spurt, Joe's company stalled, got stuck, and ultimately failed. While he had a number of highly skilled employees, their skills weren't enough to get the company over the hump. They attracted a significant amount of business during their first year of operation, but they couldn't build on it. The problem: Joe and his top people weren't aligned. The misalignment meant that when they tried to work as a team, they failed; their meetings were characterized by bickering and an inability to achieve consensus. Some of his best people were wrapped up in their egos. Others were so functionally myopic (i.e., the tech manager couldn't even bring himself to think about marketing) that they never could implement a holistic strategy that took all parts of a problem or opportunity into consideration. And on a big picture level, no one was as driven as Joe to grow the company. It wasn't just that his leadership team didn't work as hard as Joe. They made decisions based on the short-term rather than the long-term sustainability and growth of the company; they voted for taking bigger bonuses rather than investing some of that bonus money back into the company.

The outcome: the company was sold for the assumption of debt plus the below-market salaries of five remaining employees who transitioned to the acquiring company.

Now let's look at an entrepreneur who was smart about finding and hiring the right type of leaders. Carrie was a serial entrepreneur who was an early adopter of Facebook marketing. Carrie relished building companies quickly, creating a buzz about them, and then selling them; she was looking to create a company that gave her a billion dollar exit. Though Carrie was in the game for the money, she also loved the process of creating something of value to a market and she valued the learning and agility that was essential to her success.

In her most recent startup, Carrie worked with us to hire a leadership team within a three-month period. During this time, we brought in a CFO, CTO, controller, SVP client services, and a handful of other high-level managers. From the start, Carrie had great clarity about her ambitious financial goals for the company as well as her fervent belief in learning and agility and crucial traits of her top people, based on her past experiences. She made it a point to tell us that she wanted to recruit leaders who were excited about the fast-paced way she ran her companies, who relished pivoting as a volatile marketplace required adjustments, and who were eager to acquire new knowledge and skills to keep up with the rapid pace of change.

Carrie told us she wanted us to find skilled practitioners, but she agreed that she was willing to sacrifice a bit of experience and expertise for people who shared her beliefs about what was important in running and growing a startup. All the leadership-level people who we hired met Carrie's criteria, and though the company grew quickly because they had good products and excellent marketing, a lot of their success can be attributed to the alignment of their leadership team around values and mission. Sitting in on a team meeting, it was almost as if all the people at the table were communicating on a psychic level; they finished each other's sentences and when they argued, the debates were brief and resolved without bitter feelings.

Three years after the company's inception, Carrie sold it for $800 million. It didn't hit Carrie's $1 billion goal, but it seems likely that such a sale is in Carrie's future.

AVOID THE BIGGEST
ENTREPRENEURIAL MISTAKE

This is one of the biggest hires you've ever made. You have a lot riding on bringing in the right leader for your company. Perhaps it's the first time you've ever hired a CEO, COO, or CTO. Maybe you're going to give a big equity stake in the company to this executive with the idea of partnership or him buying you out at some point in the future. And it might simply be that you hope to fill this position with the person who will take the company to the next level.

Whatever the scenario is, the search and recruitment process takes on a lot more meaning for you than it would for a lesser position. In these instances, some entrepreneurs make a fatal mistake: They opt for control over profit.

Harvard Business School Professor Noam Wasserman has written about "the founder's dilemma," and it boils down to choosing to maintain great control of the company versus giving up some of this control in exchange for growth and profit. The greatest value an entrepreneur will create happens when she either becomes a leader of leaders or hires one. This takes courage. It means letting go of some control. It makes an entrepreneur vulnerable. And this can cause discomfort. When it comes to recruiting leaders, entrepreneurs often choose control. This means that they internalize the hiring process, refusing to involve or listen to other advisors. They believe that no one knows their company as well as they do, that no one has more to gain or lose based on this one hire.

Enter the board member or advisor. A board comprised of independent executives with strong operating experience will outperform a board comprised of financial engineers. I like to match entrepreneurs with board members or advisors who have real operating chops and who can help them clear personal growth hurdles. Following a structured process with input from operational-savvy board members requires relinquishing a bit of control, but it will yield far better results than relying only on one's instinct. This may seem counterintuitive to entrepreneurs, but it avoids the mistake of choosing someone who seems right but is actually wrong for a key position.

And while entrepreneurs often do have great instincts, these instincts can betray them when it comes to crucial hiring decisions. More often than not, an entrepreneur's gut tells him to hire someone who resembles himself. What's reassuring is a candidate who was raised in the same neighborhood, who is the same religion or from the same ethnic group, who went to the same school, who worked for the same company, or who has a similar personality. Without knowing it, this entrepreneur ends up hiring a clone of himself, when what he really needs is someone who brings a different perspective, set of experiences, and skills to the table.

Hiring a clone, though, fosters the illusion of control. And so it's not unusual to find entrepreneurs who hire their college buddies for top positions or people with whom they started their careers. As reassuring as this may be, these individuals often lack not only the complementary ideas and skills that are crucial to the company, but they don't share the entrepreneur's mission and values.

To avoid this situation, seek input from others about your leadership hires. Whether it's your internal executive team or outside consultants, they usually can counterbalance your unconscious desire for control. Or do what Amazon and Google do: When they are contemplating a hire, they bring in an employee from a different group or function than the position being filled and give this employee "yes" or "no" power over the hire. Consider bringing in an employee who isn't enmeshed in the function where you have a leadership opening (or someone who isn't part of your leadership team) and solicit their opinion on a candidate. This outside viewpoint will provide an objective look at a candidate and her fit in the organization; this employee isn't concerned about control issues but is focused on how a given candidate might benefit the company and help it achieve its goals.

FOUR WAYS TO HIRE THE RIGHT LEADERS AND MANAGERS

I absolutely believe that entrepreneurs can find, secure, and keep great leaders. You don't have to be General Motors or IBM to hire someone who will contribute mightily to your vision for your company. As the late radio personality Casey Kasem once said, "Keep your feet on the ground and reach for the stars." But the first part of that quote means anchoring your ambitious search in reality. If you can't afford a seven figure package for a leader, don't interview people who are in that salary stratosphere. At the same time, don't forget that you can attract an incredible executive to your company if you find a values match—people who resonate with what you're trying to do and how you're trying to do it will be drawn to your company.

With that in mind, here are four suggestions that can help you find a top executive who can help you realize your entrepreneurial vision:

Slow Down

Entrepreneurs often move quickly, many times out of necessity. The demands of running a small, nimble company often require quick decisions, and their personalities sometimes predispose them to be impatient.

Impulsive hiring is never a good idea, no matter what position you're hiring for. But it's an especially bad idea when you're looking for a leader. Therefore, slow down. I'm not talking about the time frame necessarily (sometimes you do need to hire someone quickly) but the thought process. Put everything down on paper—the skills/knowledge necessary to do the job well as well as the values/mission that are critical for a leader to have. Use the Blueprint (introduced in Chapter 5) if it helps you articulate the skills and values that are your non-negotiables. Here it is again on the next page.

Focus on the non-negotiables you require for a position—the crucial qualities beyond the job skills that you cannot do without. Discuss with your team what's most important for the company, now and in the future. Is it a brilliantly innovative mind; the ability to empathize; a willingness to develop people and help them become great at their jobs? Is one of these qualities more important than all the others? Think about the discussion and determine the top four non-negotiables. Then, when you start interviewing candidates, you know what you're looking for. By slowing your process, you are much more thoughtful and informed about what you need and are less likely to fall victim to confirmation bias: drawing quick conclusions about who you need to hire and then interviewing candidates and looking for "evidence" that support these conclusions. For instance, you determine that your new COO must be highly organized (perhaps because your last COO was poorly organized and that created headaches for everyone). You interview a candidate who is a neat freak, and he shows you his iPad which is tightly organized; he also speaks in a very precise, clear manner. But being organized isn't as important as an inclusive mindset or a willingness

CORE FIT SELECTION™
BLUEPRINT

◆◆ DAVE PARTNERS

POSITION [   ] **DATE** [   ]

COMPANY

MISSION
(What We Are Doing)

CORE VALUES
(Who We Are)

CULTURE
*(How We Do It,
What We Celebrate,
Reward & Recognize)*

ROLE

CORE COMPETENCIES	SUCCESS FACTORS	STRATEGIC OUTCOMES
1.	1.	1.
2.	2.	2.
3.	3.	3.
4.	4.	4.
5.	5.	5.

What are the Intrinsic Qualities This Person Must Possess To Be Effective?

What Must This Person Achieve To Help Drive The Strategic Outcomes?

What Are The Corporate Priorities To Be Achieved In The Next 12 Months?

CANDIDATE

Proven Experience: What Must They Have Already Achieved In Their Career & Bring To This Role?

Must Haves:	Nice To Haves:
1.	1.
	2.
2.	3.
	4.
3.	

Supervisor Name:_____ Title:_____ Signature:_____
(Who Does This Position Report To?)

For a PDF download of the Blueprint and other resources, go to
www.HireSmartFromTheStart.com

to generate affiliation among employees. This highly organized candidate might be a disaster when it comes to creating and elevating diverse teams. Slowing down before the interview will ensure that you hire for the values that are mission critical.

Distinguish Unit-Level Individual Values
from Higher-Level Core Values

Leaders are custodians and amplifiers of the company's values. When you're hiring someone to head a function, however, you can become a victim of value confusion. For instance, Tom seems like a great potential CFO hire. He's great with numbers, and has the right kind of experience handling the financial issues that pertain to your industry. And he looks like he can slide in seamlessly as a member of your financial group. Like most of the employees in finance, he's thorough, deadline-focused, and is a bit of a nerd.

While Tom may be a great fit for finance, he may not be a great fit for the company. As a leader, he needs to embrace and embody the larger values that you as an entrepreneur prize and that inform the larger culture. Is Tom a consensus-builder? Does he prioritize learning and development?

Most companies have cultures within cultures, values within values. Typically, each department or function has its own distinguishing traits or qualities that the majority of people share. If you're hiring someone at a lower level for a function, it makes sense that you want to bring in someone who fits that function. But when you hire a manager, you have to assess for higher, core values.

Find a Great Small Team Leader

When you think about it, leaders in most entrepreneurial companies are responsible for no more than eight people. Unlike a large corporation where leaders may supervise many more employees, entrepreneurial leaders tend to run relatively small, agile teams. In a big company, a leader who is cold and distant, who embodies the old command-and-control model, who is a high-level strategist but not particularly good with people, might still be effective. In a smaller, entrepreneurial setting, this type of leader will probably fail.

A great small team leader is someone who facilitates team agility, who can help the team pivot to capitalize on rapidly changing events. This leader listens to team members without prejudice. She is open to everyone's input and ideas, no matter how different they are from her own or the norm. This type of leader is also a transparent and active communicator; no one has to guess what's on her mind. Above all else, a small team leader is the champion of organization values and drives the team toward the company mission.

Sacrifice a Bit of Technical Skill
for a Lot of Value

If you're interviewing ten candidates for a leadership position and you hire the one who has absolutely the best technical qualifications for the position, you may be hiring the wrong person. I know the head of a printing company who, when hiring a vice president, maintains that he's going to look for the individual with the best combination of experience and expertise, saying, "I'm going to pay a lot of money to this person, so I'm not going to compromise with a candidate who isn't in the top 1 percent of skills and knowledge."

Like other entrepreneurs, this small business owner wants to hire the best engineer, financial expert, salesperson, and so on. And it's entirely possible that leaders in entrepreneurial companies won't just lead but will be individual contributors; they may run a team but they'll also create the budget, sell to customers, and fix the machines. Nonetheless, if that leader doesn't embody the values that the company holds sacred, then all this technical skill is for naught; he'll either leave prematurely or prevent the company from achieving its mission. Right from the search's inception, establish the level of technical chops required. More importantly, determine the underlying core competencies like intelligence, analytic capabilities, coaching, creativity, and so on.

I'm not suggesting ignoring a candidate's qualifications to do the job; you need a high level of competence. At the same time, you can make a much better hire if you choose the candidate who is the best match in terms of values and mission, even if there's a slight drop off in expertise or experience. Remember, technical chops is only up to a 20 percent determinant of whether candidates succeed. It's a tradeoff, and entrepreneurs are good at tradeoffs. You may lose a small degree of ability and gain a high degree of values.

OPTIONS TO HIRING A LEADER

At this point, let's pause and ask a question that might be on your mind: Why do you have to hire a top executive; why can't you just promote from within?

After considering the advice I've offered, you may wonder about whether investing time and energy in recruiting the right leader is worth it. Perhaps you're dubious about all the interviews you need to conduct to locate someone who isn't just technically skilled but has congruent mission and values. Perhaps you're worried about the expense of bringing in a high-level person to your company.

If so, let's consider your options to recruiting an outside leader:

- **Promoting an existing manager to a top position.** This is the ideal solution . . . if you have an ideal candidate ready and waiting. Most entrepreneurs don't. It may be that you need to replace someone who left suddenly when she received a great offer from another company. Or you've experienced a sudden growth spurt and need someone who has the experience and expertise to lead a fast-growing team. The odds are that you haven't had the opportunity to groom an internal candidate or that the person with the skills and experience you require doesn't exist in your company.

- **Training an internal candidate for the role.** Again, this is a great idea with two big IFs—IF you have the time and IF you have an employee with the skills and values crucial for a top job. Most leaders are made, not born. Even if you have a great executive development program, it can require months or longer to prepare someone to become a COO or CMO. In addition, you may have highly skilled individual contributors—people who are incredible salespeople or experts at finance or brilliant techies—but there's no guarantee that that these skills mean they'll do well when promoted to positions of great responsibility.

- **Stepping in and doing it yourself.** This is often an entrepreneurial reflex. Your CFO leaves and you say to yourself, I'm good with the numbers, I can handle these tasks for a while. Maybe you can. But at what cost to the company? Whatever you're best at—strategy, creating new products, and so on—is diminished when you spend an increasing amount of time in a role that is secondary to your main contributions.

- **Doing nothing.** This is the default option. Entrepreneurs are often so busy with the quotidian details of work that they figure that they can get by without a functional group leader or other top executive and that everyone will pitch in and compensate for the missing leader. They rationalize that they don't have the time or the budget to recruit someone, that they'll see how things go and if necessary, start looking for someone at some point in the future. The problem, of course, is that in the interim things can go to hell in a handbasket; and at the point you decide you need to fill a leader position, you're going to be facing a delay of weeks or months before you can identify candidates, interview them, make an offer, and have it accepted.

Let me be clear about all these options: I'm not telling you they're bad. For some of you, they represent the right thing to do at a given moment in time, based on your circumstances. I should also state the obvious: I have a horse in this race. As an executive recruiter, I'm naturally biased in favor of recruiting leaders.

But my bias is based on years of experience. I believe in a world of abundance, not scarcity. When you try to fill a critical position in your company from a shallow pool—your existing employees— you may not find what you're looking for. But if you search far and wide, your pool is much deeper. Every day, I'm amazed anew by how much talent exists, and by how many viable candidates are available for just about every entrepreneurial company at every job level.

Therefore, consider all your options, but don't neglect the option of searching for a leader from the abundance of talent that's out there.

THE THREE KEY QUALITIES YOU CAN'T DO WITHOUT . . . AND HOW TO IDENTIFY THEM

All entrepreneurial companies have different leadership needs. A billion-dollar tech startup looking for a CEO has different requirements than a small chain of automobile repair shops searching for the same position. If you're looking for a top functional manager, you need to tailor your search to experience and expertise within that function. Similarly, startups with hyper-aggressive growth cultures need to find leaders who are somewhat different in values and mission than slower growth, family-oriented operations.

Nonetheless, entrepreneurial enterprises of every size and cultural type share certain things. They all face an increasingly volatile environment and must be prepared to make changes quickly. They all exist in a world overflowing with emerging knowledge, where new technologies, processes, strategies, marketing, and other developments require a willingness to learn. They will all only attract and retain the best people if employees feel included and valued.

Leaders who are capable of addressing the following three factors are invaluable to every entrepreneurial company. Let's look at these factors and how to identify them in leadership candidates:

1. Agility

You may be able to get away with hiring an individual contributor who's somewhat rigid in his outlook and habits. But when it comes to a leader, agility is crucial. Think about your business and how it's buffeted by change. For today's entrepreneur, everything is in flux— your products, services, processes, and technologies. The ability to pivot in the face of change—to be able to adjust a familiar way of working to take advantage of a new development—is something you want in your leaders at all levels and in all functions.

But how do you know if a candidate possesses this agility? While it's impossible to know for sure until you work with her, the following questions can help you probe whether she was agile in the past and is likely to be agile in the future:

- Have you ever managed a team where your approach to a problem wasn't working? How did you respond to help the team become more effective?
- Can you describe an instance when you had to make a 180 degree shift in policy or strategy; where you had to try something completely different in response to changes internally or externally?
- How have you changed as a leader over the years? How have you adjusted your management style and leadership persona from your first leadership job to now? Why did you make these shifts and how challenging was it to make them?

2. Hunger for Learning

If you're interviewing a candidate who is set in his ways, who thinks he knows everything, who dismisses new methods out of hand, then this is not someone you want to hire, no matter how sterling his other credentials might be. Every entrepreneurial company operates in data-rich environments. New developments in technology, manufacturing methods, governmental regulations and so on create a neverending stream of data. More to the point, all this data can be sifted for information and knowledge—information and knowledge that can help companies solve problems and take advantage of opportunities. Many times, it can yield a new and better way of doing things—from maintaining a customer relationship to entering a new market.

Even the sleepiest, most secure, most local ma-and-pa business must pay attention to all of this information and capitalize on it. In a global, interconnected work environment, entrepreneurs must learn or die. Leaders are the chief learning officers of entrepreneurial companies. They are the ones who must keep their eyes trained on all sectors of the outside world and monitor them for relevant events, trends, and knowledge.

Here are some questions that will help you identify a candidate who hungers to learn:

- In your current job, do you actively monitor developments in relevant business sectors that might affect your company? What system do you have in place to monitor these developments?
- Do you feel as if you're innately curious? Do you like reading from a diversity of print and online publications about your business? Do you subscribe to a variety of publications and newsletters and attend industry workshops and conferences?
- What is the single most important thing you've learned in the past year that has helped you be a more effective leader?

3. Humility

If I were to name a single trait that you should look for when interviewing top managerial or leadership candidates, humility would be at the top of the list (though here, I saved the best for last). This may not strike you as the trait that you'd put at the top of your list, but bear with me as I make my case.

First, let's define humility. It is a virtue characterized by a modest view of your own importance. You still have a healthy ego; you still maintain your confidence. But you're open to the importance of others, to the value of other opinions and ideas.

In an entrepreneurial environment, humility offers many advantages. Think about the chaotic, fast-paced nature of the work environment at times. Leaders who are arrogant tend to become hot-tempered and impatient during these times. They alienate their people. They don't listen to concepts outside of their comfort zones. Humble leaders, on the other hand, are patient and trusting, even when they're under stress. As deadlines approach and pressure is applied, they become even more inclusive in their decision making. They are more focused on the best idea to solve a problem rather than being the one who comes up with the best idea.

Leaders with humility also are able to manage the risk that comes with entrepreneurship. Keith Cunningham, my leadership mentor, notes that risk in business is inversely proportional to the perception of its existence. All leaders are one bad decision away from total calamity. The greater the perception that there is no risk, the more likely that risk will hurt the business in some way. Arrogance and overinflated egos make entrepreneurs especially vulnerable to risk; that same close-minded certainty, foolish bravado, and hubris caused the cataclysmic catastrophes at Enron, Barings Bank, and Lehman Brothers.

With humility, leaders are willing to acknowledge risk. They are attuned to how marketplace forces and their own decisions can increase risk, and they have the sense not to make decisions that create too much exposure to risk.

Thilo Semmelbauer of Shutterstock is one of the most successful leaders in the New York tech world. While he holds himself to high personal standards, he represents the professional virtues of compassion, empathy, and authenticity well. His humility has contributed mightily to this success. "I'm personally not sure if 'humility' per se contributed to my success. I never thought about it this way. I simply believe that you can't do it alone, and that in order to get people on board with you, you have to listen, be open, and be willing to change directions when better ideas emerge. Maybe I'm just pragmatic." Thilo took WeightWatchers.com from zero to over $400 million, and then ran all global operations for Weight Watchers (over \$1.6 billion revenue) before I recruited him to Ladders. I only worked with Thilo for a few months before leaving to hang up my own shingle at Dave Partners and Thilo left a few months after that to run the business at Shutterstock. As I mentioned earlier, Thilo helped grow the Shutterstock business from \$60 million to an IPO to more than \$400 million in revenues. He is a leader in the true sense of the word and beloved by all.

He is an active listener, totally dedicated to his teams, and truly open to learning from the people he works with. He never thinks he's the only one with the answers. If he comes up with a plan or a strategy, he is open to change if someone else has a good suggestion. Because he is honest and transparent, people aren't intimidated by him. Instead, they feel he is someone they can talk to, and someone who will listen to them.

How do you identify Thilo-like humility in leadership candidates? Here are key questions to ask:

- As confident as you are in your own ideas and decisions, do you encourage others to challenge them? Can you describe a situation where you recognized that someone else's idea was better than your own and opted to do what they suggested?
- Have you ever been described as arrogant? If so, do you feel that term was unfair? Why might someone have described you this way?
- Is your office door always open, literally and figuratively? Do people routinely stop by to talk, to make suggestions, to offer constructive criticism? Are you able to manage your ego when you feel your authority is being challenged and refrain from using position power to stifle this challenge?

CHAPTER 10

Finding and Recruiting People Who Get Things Done

E ntrepreneurs know the value of employees who can cut through the red tape, meet tight deadlines, make the sale, and fix the problem. Small business owners have told me that they can't afford to hire brilliant people who are not so brilliant at implementation. Unlike big corporations, they can't afford to carry employees who are smart and talented but not particularly productive.

The challenge, though, is identifying who is a producer and who is not during the search and recruitment process. Job candidates always claim that they are good at getting things done. But separating doers from talkers isn't simple. It's actually more complex than you might believe, since the person who is great at executing tasks in one entrepreneurial organization probably won't be great in another company.

To understand what execution really means—especially what it means to entrepreneurs—we need to look at why people perform so well in certain situations and not others.

THE THREE FACTORS
AFFECTING EXECUTION

Most employees want to get things done. Unfortunately, they're not always in the right job, environment, or point in their career to be good at executing tasks. It's a mistake to divide the world into doers and non-doers, to believe that some are great at working hard and productively and others aren't. It's a much more complex issue than this.

Consider Laurie. Ten years ago, a small software company hired her as a salesperson. It was Laurie's second job; she had worked for a startup for little more than a year before it went under. The owner liked Laurie; the company was in an industry dominated by men at the time and the owner was happy to find another woman who seemed to be qualified for the position. The owner and Laurie got along great and became friends, but before the year was up, the owner fired her. Laurie struggled to sell the company's products, and as much as the owner liked her, it was obvious that she wasn't producing.

Over the next nine years, Laurie had a series of sales jobs with tech companies, including one of the largest in the field as well as smaller ones. About a year ago, Laurie landed a job with a software company on a fast-growth path because of their highly sophisticated products. Almost from the start, Laurie excelled and quickly became the company's star salesperson. Her boss remarked that he wouldn't trade Laurie for any salesperson in the world because she understood their products, knew the best way to sell them, and was especially adept at closing tough-to-close deals.

How had Laurie gone from someone who couldn't get things done to someone who could? Part of it was experience and expertise—she developed that over the years between these two jobs. Part of it was that her boss at her current job and the company itself were ideally suited to Laurie and she to them: She relished working for a high-growth company and for a boss whose beliefs and values mirrored her own; and she was given the autonomy she craved, allowed to sell the way she wanted.

While I believe that people should have total ownership and accountability for what they take on, sometimes structural deficiencies exist when people fail to execute. They usually aren't "flawed" in some way—lazy, satisfied with mediocrity, indecisive—but are hampered by one or more of the following:

1. Don't have the knowledge/skills/experience. They're not producing because they just don't know enough to do the job effectively. Obviously, people who are just starting out in their careers are most likely to be affected by this problem, but it can also be an issue for more veteran employees. For instance, you assume that someone knows how to do a given task because they've been working in the field for a while, but it's possible that they've never had to do this task before, or they received inadequate training in how to do it. Employees often are embarrassed to admit that they don't know how to do something that they feel they should know, and this is where they may assume a mask during interviews. But all you see is that they don't seem to be getting things done, and you assume the problem is laziness or inability. In fact, if employees have strong learning potential, they can probably be trained relatively quickly and change from non-producer to producer.

2. Don't have the "want to." It's not that they're inherently unmotivated; it's that they're working at a company that's providing them with the wrong motivation. For instance, companies exist where the prime motivation is money. That's fine; I'm not making a judgment. Some people are primarily motivated by profit, and if they land at this type of company, they'll probably be motivated to work hard and well. Others, however, are motivated by other things: a chance to make a difference, changing a product category or industry, helping others learn and grow. Some people respond positively when they're in a culture that mirrors their values; they have a sense of affiliation and that feeling drives them to work harder and better. When you're in the right place, you're intrinsically motivated to solve problems, capitalize on opportunities, and do whatever it takes to meet or exceed objectives.

3. Don't have the authority. Sometimes, employees aren't in a position to get things done. They aren't given sufficient responsibility or resources. They are placed in difficult situations where they don't receive the go-ahead for any ideas that deviate from the norm. They may be doers, but they're denied the authority or ability to execute in ways that makes sense to them. Consequently, they fall short of expectations, either because they're lacking the funds or the backing necessary to do something the way they feel is correct.

Given these three factors, don't set people up to fail inadvertently by the way you recruit. If, like many entrepreneurs, you're focused on hiring employees who seem like doers, then you probably will recruit looking for qualities such as:

- Assertiveness
- Drive
- Self-starter
- Ambitious
- Goal-oriented
- Take-charge personality

There's nothing wrong with any of these qualities, except they may fool you into believing you hired a doer when you have not. Of much greater importance is answering the following questions during the recruiting process:

Does the candidate possess the technical chops and more? This is the most obvious question and the one you are most likely to ask. But go beyond the usual assumptions—he had a job before as a CFO so he should be able to handle your CFO job—and think about what the job really requires. Is it the ability to negotiate with tough-minded people? Is it a keen analytical sense? There are the technical specs, and then there are the traits that really help people accomplish a lot in a given position.

Does the candidate have high learning, growth, and expansion potential? People with the hunger to learn and the ability to soak up expertise will become doers. They just won't always hit the ground running. Entrepreneurs may seek this learning potential in young people applying for their first or second jobs, but it's equally important in more veteran employees. Entrepreneurial companies vary widely; they are reflections of their founders, and each founder has certain idiosyncrasies and visions that are distinct. As a result, any new employee will have a lot to learn. Liza Landsman, executive vice president of Jet.com, said, "I really like people who are insatiably intellectually curious. To me that's the signal of people who are lifelong learners and who will be open to learning from each other and from their own teams." Steve Johnson, the recent chief revenue officer of Hootsuite, would deliver similar advice to his younger self if he could: "I would be *much* more aware that you don't have to know it all and that it's completely fine to ask lots and lots of questions and get advice early." To assess learning potential, see if candidates are naturally inquisitive during interviews. Do they ask you a lot of good questions? Are they eager to discuss new techniques, theories, and ideas they've heard about?

Is the candidate likely to be motivated by our mission and values? If there's a match (between the candidate's beliefs, goals, and work-style and those of the company), then it's likely that this individual will be driven to accomplish tasks at a high level. During the interview process, focus on what really makes the candidate tick; what gets her excited and engaged about her work; why she worked so hard on a project in the past and the satisfaction she derived from this experience. Does the candidate get most excited when she talks about her record-setting commission or how she helped the company achieve record-setting growth? Does she relish the synergy of great teams or individual accomplishment?

Is the candidate intrinsically or extrinsically motivated? In school, some students try to get great grades to please parents, meet teachers' expectations, or to get into good colleges; others try to get excellent marks because they are driven to do so for their own sake—they hold themselves to a high standard. Similarly, some employees are motivated by bonuses, titles, and approval of the boss. Others are focused on doing the best they possibly can. It's not that they don't want to be rewarded, but that they can't tolerate giving anything less than their best effort; they feel good knowing that they tried as hard as they could.

Will the candidate have sufficient influence and authority to achieve ambitious goals? When you're talking to candidates about what the position requires and how you'll measure performance, are you being realistic? Entrepreneurs, often out of necessity, try to squeeze as much performance out of their people as possible. But are you willing to provide a given candidate the clout to do what you're asking? Are you willing to allow her to take certain risks and make decisions with autonomy? Maybe you feel comfortable providing this support to more senior candidates, but not to others?

Are you willing and able to supply a given candidate with the resources necessary to execute effectively? Essentially, this means people and budgets. Can you provide your candidate with the human resources and dollars necessary to accomplish the tasks you set forth? As you know better than anyone, entrepreneurial businesses can be volatile. In good times, you can answer this question affirmatively. In tough times, it's more difficult to do so. You may have the best of intentions, but when you hire the candidate and business conditions become worse, you may have to cut back on the resources you provide.

These questions are all designed to help you not only hire candidates who can get things done, but to be realistic about the standards to which they're held. Employees need to be in the right situations to get things done at high levels. Therefore, make sure you're finding candidates who can thrive in your company and who have all the power and support they need to produce great results.

WHAT KIND OF DOER DO YOU WANT TO HIRE?

There are different ways to get things done. Tailoring your candidate search to the particular kind of doer you need is crucial. Here's a simple analogy that gets this point across. One company needs to hire a carpenter who is brilliant at hammering all types of nails straight and true. Another company is looking for a manager who can run a team that is charged with finding a better way to hammer nails. A third company is searching for a leader who can inspire others to hammer nails faster and better than other companies in their category.

Before beginning your search, consider which of the following doer types you want to hire:

- An individual contributor who has the knowledge and skills to handle specific job tasks
- An individual contributor who can get things done very quickly
- An individual contributor who is able to accomplish tasks with a high degree of quality
- An individual contributor who is willing to work as many hours as it takes to meet objectives
- A manager who knows how to run teams that accomplish objectives
- A manager who gets things done as both an individual contributor and a supervisor
- A leader who delivers results indirectly by coming up with great ideas and strategies that others implement
- A leader who creates a sense of mission and camaraderie that motivates people to work hard and well

Speaking of leaders, if you're hiring for a senior managerial position, recognize that your own doing style will impact the type of doer you hire. Mark is the head of a family-owned retail chain, and he is the quintessential roll-up-your-sleeves, do-it-yourself leader. He pitches in inspecting inventory and even stocking the shelves.

If needed, he'll even work the cash registers at one of the company's five stores. Nancy, on the other hand, is the founder of an alternative health products company, and she focuses almost all her time on research into cutting-edge products and selecting the ones the company will offer on its website. She rarely participates in the daily activities of running the company.

The lesson: Know your doer style as a leader and seek a complementary leader or manager. When I was at Ladders, there were two leadership teams. On one, there were Alex and Leslie. Alex was a creative visionary, and Leslie was terrific at nuts-and-bolts implementation of ideas. The other team was headed by myself and Angela. I was the innovative headhunter and she the operational human resources executive. Together as leaders, our two teams helped grow the business to $85 million in revenues in five years. To create that growth, we were constantly getting things done—executing great strategies with astonishing, complementary effectiveness.

The key was what authors Gino Wickman and Mark C. Winters refer to as "ying and yang" in their book, *Rocket Fuel*. They believe that the critical combination of one leader who is a Visionary and another who is an Integrator helps accomplish highly ambitious business goals. As talented as these individuals might be, it's only when they start working together that they produce tremendous results.

Most of you know this principle intuitively. In your company, you possess front stage and back stage employees. The former people are the face of the organization, meeting with customers and suppliers, blogging, making speeches, setting the strategy. The latter individuals work behind the scenes, balancing the books, creating the software, analyzing the data. Without one group, the other would be ineffective.

The same holds true for your leadership team. Unfortunately, during the hiring process many entrepreneurs seek people who they like and get along with—whose personalities mesh with theirs. Typically, these individuals share similarities when it comes to how they get things done—they both are aggressive, idea-spouting risk-takers who love to push the boundaries. Yet odds are, they probably won't get a lot done together. They probably will have great lunches and conversations, but they won't do the research, planning, and follow-up that helps put their brilliant ideas into action.

Consider the stereotypical entrepreneur. This is someone who has ADD, who has a million thoughts bouncing around in his head. He doesn't have much patience for long meetings and drawn-out testing phases; he hates all the talk and loves all the action. If this entrepreneur hires a "crony" as his number two person, he will lack a counterpart who can make sense of his ideas, who can raise objections and tell him no, who can help the entrepreneur figure out what's worth pursuing and how to pursue it efficiently.

The simple rule of hiring another leader who can help you implement your ideas: Seek your complementary counterpart, not your clone.

HOW VALUES TRANSLATE INTO ACTION

Yes, to find someone who can get things done, you want to focus on experience—has a candidate done what you want her to do? It's wise, too, to assess whether she possesses other qualities—agility, an eagerness to learn, and so on—that facilitate achievement in entrepreneurial settings.

The most important factor, though, is values. While you may buy the need for a values fit as a recruiting tool, you may wonder if it really applies when it comes to productivity. After all, your most productive people may be individuals whose values don't fit with yours, but who work hard, meet every deadline, and do quality work.

Let me suggest, though, that entrepreneurs sometimes set the productivity bar too low. More accurately, they measure the wrong things.

It's not what you get done that counts: it's getting the right things done. Entrepreneur Mark Suster wrote a terrific and widely read blog titled, *Doing the Right Thing > Doing Things Right*. He has a great analogy in the blog: "It's the parable of the tree-chopping team that is so focused on efficiency of how fast it can fell a tree that it doesn't bother to make sure it is clearing the forest in the right direction when one person actually stops the constant cutting to climb a tree and make sure they're cutting in the right direction. On the surface this person is losing efficiency but in the long run the gains for direction setting are huge."

Employees exist in your company who always seem to be doing things, but have you ever considered if they are doing things that are furthering your company's mission and goals? Or are they accomplishing tasks that may be necessary but are more quotidian than mission-focused? Yes, it's important to fill out the financial spreadsheets, but it's much more important to devise a financial strategy that will help the company achieve its five-year plan.

When you're recruiting, you can't always tell if a candidate will be capable of doing the right things just by looking at his resume or even through extensive interviewing. You may have a good sense and make a good hire based on these factors alone, but you should take one more step. The only way to know for sure is by assessing his values and mission. If they're in synch with yours, then it's highly likely that he'll focus reflexively on tasks that are integral to what you want to achieve in the long run. If, for instance, you're driven to attain a market leadership position in your category in five years, you need employees who possess that same vision. In that way, they will automatically tailor their work to fit the ultimate goal rather than a less essential (though more easily achievable) one. Similarly, if you value creating a company where learning and innovation thrive, you need to hire someone who also embodies these qualities. These values will guide their actions; they will be most productive in areas related to learning and innovation. You can count on them to put forth all their effort and ingenuity to achieve objectives related to these values.

The most practical entrepreneurs may wonder if they can afford to assess candidates for mission and values, since they are more concerned about getting work done today than realizing their future vision for the company. They feel pressure to pay back investors, and so they want to hire people who will help them do so immediately. But if you bring in employees who share your mission and values, they will not only provide this immediate productivity on basic and essential tasks but also work toward achieving bigger objectives.

HOW DO PEOPLE AT YOUR COMPANY GET THINGS DONE?

This is a serious question, and one that pertains to your culture. Answering it will help you determine the odds a new employee has of being productive, no matter what her skills might be.

In cultures where learning, experimentation, and a focus on excellence predominate, new hires tend to be productive faster than in other companies. In these companies, people feel comfortable asking questions when they don't know the answers or taking their time to figure out the solution to a problem instead of pretending to know what to do. They also are encouraged to test new ideas and approaches rather than "do things the way we do them around here." And they recognize that aiming high and being conscientious about work are key values; they know that excellence isn't just a word given lip service, but a living, breathing reality of the company.

This is opposed to a culture of what I term, "false harmony." Here, entrepreneurs try to build "kumbaya" enterprises where conflict is absent and employees are coddled. Obviously, this isn't the old-school entrepreneurial company. But it is a culture I've seen in some startups where idealistic founders are heavily focused on creating camaraderie and consensus, assuming this will lead to results.

It doesn't. Instead, data and deadlines often go by the wayside. No one wants to get bogged down by metrics or stress-inducing short time frames. No one wants to impose their structures or ideas on others. It's all very egalitarian, and it may create a false harmony where no one is angry and everyone enjoys working at the company. But it's tough to generate results when metrics aren't enforced and where people don't debate, sometimes acrimoniously, to arrive at a solution.

Disruptive innovation isn't always nice or pretty. It can get messy when someone ventures a provocative idea that shakes up everyone. People don't like to let go of cherished notions or treasured ways of conducting business. But disruptive ideas can pave the way for great results; they give doers a chance to shine.

Therefore, before making a hire based on who will fit into your culture, you need to think long and hard—and talk with your top people—about whether your culture will allow the great implementer you're thinking of hiring to get stuff done.

CHAPTER 11

Your
First Hire

Bringing Entrepreneurial Energy
and Agility to a New Skill Set

M any entrepreneurs, no matter how savvy they are about business, have relatively little recruiting experience. If this describes you, join the club. It may be that you were always too busy with other business issues to get deeply involved in the hiring process. It may be that until your recent growth spurt, your company didn't have many hiring needs. It may be that you've emigrated recently from the corporate world and always had human resources professionals to help with your people requirements. And of course, it's possible that you've recently opened your first business and have never needed to hire anyone before.

Whatever your situation, it's possible that you have little experience with some or all of the three stages of the recruitment process: sourcing, screening, and securing. While all of our previous discussion may have prepared you for these three stages, you may be lacking some of the knowledge and nuances that only come when you've enmeshed yourself in recruiting candidates.

To help you gain the information necessary to make a good hire, let's look at what happens as you move through the recruiting process and the skills you need at each stage.

THE TASKS CHANGE BUT
THE GOAL REMAINS THE SAME

Consider recruiting within the context of volume and skill. In the sourcing stage, the key tasks require high volume and low skill. More specifically, you're identifying scores or even hundreds of candidates through various means, but you don't have to be particularly discerning at this stage about which candidate makes the best fit. In the screening stage, you must exhibit a higher level of skill as the volume goes down; you have to be astute about whether a candidate meets the job's technical requirements as well as if they seem like they'd be a good match for your company, given your mission and values. Through interviewing, you reduce the list of candidates to a much smaller group of qualified individuals.

In the securing stage, the volume is low but the skill is high. Here, how good you are as a recruiter can result in hiring a great candidate who will mean a lot to your enterprise . . . or in losing that candidate to someone else. You may say the wrong thing during a discussion with your candidate of choice and turn her off. You may make a hire based on your gut rather than a thoughtful, values-driven process and bring in someone you get along with but who contributes little to the company.

Perhaps the biggest problem for neophyte recruiters is that they lose sight of the essential humanness of the process. They focus primarily or exclusively on a candidate's qualifications for the job; they attempt to sell the candidate by offering a high salary, perks, or titles. What they fail to do, though, is connect with the candidate on a personal level. This doesn't mean just being buddy-buddy during an interview. It means making the effort to find out what a candidate really cares about, what he hopes to achieve in his job, his career, his life. And it means responding to that personal mission by sharing what the company's mission is, and exploring whether there is a match.

It also means being sufficiently empathic that you put yourself in a candidate's shoes and anticipate what's going through her mind as she considers your offer. When I first started out, I didn't realize the importance of seeing things from a candidate's perspective. One of my first major hires was for an IT vice president at a startup, and I moved through sourcing to screening without a hitch. I found a guy, we'll call him Jerry, who seemed extraordinarily well-suited to the startup, both in terms of his skills and his fit in the culture. In fact, during my last meeting with Jerry, I was given the go-ahead to offer him the job, and he accepted.

Done deal. Only it wasn't. I failed to prepare Jerry for what might happen during his exit interview, especially given who he was and his value to his current employer. I simply assumed that he would tell them he was leaving. Instead, when he told them he was resigning to take another job, he expressed regret that he was departing and talked about how much he had enjoyed working there. To his boss, it seemed as if he were leaving the door open a crack—this wasn't his conscious intent, but it's how it sounded. The boss put together a new compensation package for Jerry and leveraged their personal relationship: He made Jerry feel guilty about leaving. Jerry eventually opted to stay with his company and reneged on his acceptance.

This was my fault, a result of my inexperience. I should have prepared him for his exit interview, instructing him to state definitely that he was leaving, both in writing and verbally. Without this instruction, Jerry acted like he was asking his boss for permission to leave.

The lesson I learned was never to neglect the human element. To secure candidates—especially talented, in-demand ones—you need to take into consideration their personalities, their positions, and their hopes and dreams. Essentially, you need to manage the process until they formally accept your offer and they show up for work in their new role on day 1.

A RECRUITING CHECKLIST

Entrepreneurs who are heavily involved in recruiting develop a mental checklist of tasks that will help ensure good hires. They recognize that recruiting the right person for a job—especially an important job—is more difficult than it might appear. As a result, they know their involvement has to be process-driven and address key issues from the time they start searching until they secure the candidate of their choice.

While this list becomes second nature to entrepreneurs who do a lot of recruiting, some of the steps may not even occur to you if you've never been heavily involved in hiring people for your company. Here are six recruiting to-dos that will help you effectively undertake what is often neglected or addressed improperly:

1. **Raise the candidate's enthusiasm levels.** Sell emotionally, not just factually. Let yourself be enthusiastic and even passionate when talking about the company and the opportunity for the candidate who takes the position. Some entrepreneurs may think allowing emotion into the conversation isn't professional. In most big corporate settings, the human resources people might

agree. But entrepreneurial environments are smaller, culturally more cohesive entities. To use a cliché, entrepreneurs treat people like family. A job isn't just a job to most candidates; it represents more than a way to make money. For some, it's a chance to make a difference. For others, it's an opportunity to learn and grow. For others, it provides a place of affiliation and inclusion. Don't fake emotion when you speak to candidates, but you should be genuine and speak from the heart about the company.

2. **Provide an intellectual spark.** The previous point doesn't mean you should make the entire pitch emotional. Balance it with a description of what about the job will challenge candidates. What will the job help them learn? How it will help them meet their career goals? What's the most difficult aspect of the job? The most rewarding?

3. **Evaluate technical chops against 100 percent of what is required for the role.** Think in advance about the level of expertise you want a candidate to possess. Don't make the mistake of simply comparing candidates against each other because you might hire the best candidate and still only achieve 60 percent of the technical chops required. Aim high when it comes to the knowledge, competencies, and experience you're targeting.

4. **Seek a core values fit.** I've said it before and I'll say it again: Mapping a candidate's personal DNA against the ability to amplify the cultural DNA of your organization requires you to think about these issues in advance of making your choice. Which candidate is best suited to carry out your company's mission and which one best reflects your values?

5. **Assess compensation and market analysis.** Before interviewing the first candidates, design an offer and structure it in a way that

will work for you AND for the finally selected candidate. This is the key to maximizing your talent acquisition strategy. Get external market data on a compensation range for your target hire and validate this along the process of interviewing different candidates. Put together a final financial compensation package that is reflective of both the market comparables as well as the level of expertise this candidate possesses.

6. **Create a closing strategy.** This is the most sensitive part of the entire recruitment process and most offers are delivered with the blunt sensitivity of a fast food happy meal; or, as in my story, without preparing your choice adequately so that you make sure he doesn't turn down your offer.

Here's an "extra credit" exercise that you might also consider integrating in your "to-do" list as you get ready to embark on your closing recruiting pitch:

Have finalist candidates present a 90-day plan *before* you make an offer. After the second or third interview, inform candidates that they're in the running for the job and that you'd like them to prepare a roadmap for hitting the ground running. They are free to ask deep questions and reconnect with anyone they've already met. Creating this plan in advance of the final offer will help them and you visualize success together. It will help set proper expectations on budget, resources, and performance metrics. It will clarify the social contracts, fact finding, and collaborative capabilities necessary to get stuff done and will raise enthusiasm levels for what is possible. You will be able to discern how much time and care they've taken for preparation of this presentation. And, most of all, it will give you a sense of their professional virtues, values, and mission alignment.

CLOSING A SALE:
MAKING A HIGHLY PERSONAL, HIGHLY THOUGHTFUL ARGUMENT

Closing is not only the most sensitive part of the process, but it's the one that entrepreneurs often take for granted. Hubris is a danger, especially for business owners whose pride in their companies may blind them to how others see those companies. Lois, for instance, runs a medium-sized family business, and she's helped it double in size over the past five years. Because the business has been consistently profitable, she has been able to provide her employees with great benefits—daycare for kids, an exercise room, generous vacation policies, and so on. Lois believes that her company is a tremendous place to work and that people are lucky to work there.

Lois was involved in the recruitment process for a sales manager, and after interviewing a number of candidates, she had decided that Marcia was an ideal fit for the company. She made an offer to Marcia during their third interview, and rather than accepting immediately, Marcia asked Lois a number of questions about commission increases if her group met or exceeded quotas as well as about senior leadership position opportunities if Marcia performed well. Lois had expected Marcia to jump at the offer, which she felt was generous. Consequently, she avoided answering Marcia's questions directly, offering only a vague assurance that if things went well, Marcia would be compensated fairly. She also kept repeating how Marcia was going to love working for the company, how it was a great environment, and how Marcia would be supervising great people.

Marcia told Lois she needed to think about it for a few days and talk to her family. When she got back to Lois, she explained that she had decided to turn the offer down and take a position with a larger company that would give her more opportunities to advance.

You're not going to secure every candidate you seek, but you will have a much higher batting average if you listen hard to candidates during the close, anticipate what their concerns or conflicts might be, and respond to them. Listen especially attentively to how candidates hope to develop within your company. If you're hiring for an individual contributor position, determine if the candidate expects opportunities to develop more expertise and experience—a reasonable goal—or if he anticipates being developed as a manager or a leader. If that isn't your intent, then you must make clear what this candidate can expect so that there isn't a disconnect in expectations from the start. Similarly, it's a red flag if a leader or manager anticipates technical development when you hope she'll grow as a leader.

To close the deal, never forget that the individual you're courting may be in high demand. Either she's already got a good job or she's received (or is likely to receive) more than one offer. If you're hiring for an important position, you're probably pursuing someone who has a significant amount of expertise and experience. Given this, you need to close with a bang and not a whimper. Follow a time tested process for reading their emotional data and securing their commitment. Here are three suggestions about how to do so:

Preempt the Counteroffer

Anticipate that someone—the candidate's current employer, other companies—will try to keep or hire the person you want. It's great if you can offer this candidate a terrific compensation package, but as I've discussed, this isn't necessarily what's going to clinch the deal. Instead, you can preempt the counteroffer during the close by asking the candidate these three questions:

1. Do you *know* what the role is and what it will take to be successful? Do you have a full understanding of this role?
2. Do you *think* you can have high success in the role? Can you do the job?
3. Do you *want* the role? Do you want to do this job?

By asking these questions and receiving affirmative responses, you remind the candidate why the job you're offering is the best job.

In addition, expect that the candidate's employer, upon hearing that he's departing, will fight to keep the employee. To win the fight, describe all of the possible and impossible terms that their boss will offer to keep them. Be relentless until they say something like, "I would never take a counteroffer!" or "Even if they offered me the moon and the stars, I wouldn't stay" or "They're not likely to do that and I wouldn't stay even if they did."

During the close, you're inoculating the candidate against whatever offer his employer makes (or an offer someone else makes). By telling the candidate what the offer might be in the most optimistic terms possible—i.e., suggesting the highest salary that might be part of a counteroffer—you make it much more difficult for that offer to have a significant impact. For one thing, the offer won't be a surprise; you've discussed it with the candidate. For another, the candidate has told you that he won't accept it; most people will honor their word. For a third, the counteroffer the candidate receives may be less than the grandiose picture you've painted; it will be underwhelming and he'll reject it.

Deliver the Tangible Offer with Impact

By the close, you should have an understanding of what is most important to your final candidate. Focus on the candidate's priorities rather than your own. Too often, entrepreneurs try to close by talking about themselves and their companies while ignoring what's top-of-mind for the candidate. Delivering the offer with impact means in the right order (from the candidate's mindset) and in the fullest of value. If cash is the most important tangible aspect of the offer for the candidate, discuss that first. If the offer is $200,000 base salary with a 30 percent bonus, talk about it as cash compensation of $260,000 on a $200,000 base. The very first number is the one that sticks in her mind. Then discuss the other things you're offering— benefits package, travel, title, and so on. Get the order of the offer presentation right and also the presentation of the offer.

Map the Future

In the close, this is what should have the most impact on candidates. Many great athletes visualize their success before their performance. Likewise, help candidates picture what life on the job will be like in the coming months and years. What will life look like working with colleagues, building a team, and performing their best work? Help them project how as they grow in the job and with the company, they will fulfill their personal mission and work according to the values they hold dear.

COMMON ROOKIE MISTAKES

Everyone makes mistakes, even the most experienced recruiters. Over time and with the learning that comes from doing something repeatedly, these mistakes become less and less frequent. But you can also avoid mistakes if you know what they are and keep them in mind as you're sourcing, screening, and securing candidates. Let's review the major errors and what you can do to avoid committing them:

Winging It

As I've emphasized earlier, you can't recruit by the seat of your pants. Some entrepreneurs learn this lesson the hard way; they wing it and end up with an employee who is ill-suited to the job or the company. After making this mistake a few times, business owners wise up and start using a more formal process to find the people they seek. As important as entrepreneurs' gut instincts are to their decision making, this is an area that often defies instinct. During all three states—sourcing, screening, and securing—rely on a formal process. In this way, you're not making a hiring decision based on a "false positive," a deceptively strong feeling about a candidate based on personal traits rather than professional and mission value. Admittedly, it's tough to resist false positives, especially if you've never been involved in recruiting employees in the past. As counterintuitive as it may be, focus on skills, values, and mission fit in a structured, logical manner.

Hunting for the Zeborsecamuña

As you might have figured out, this word is an amalgam of zebra, horse, camel, and vicuña. As you also know, this creature doesn't exist. Neither does the perfect candidate. You may want to hire a marketing executive who has twenty-five years experience in a given area, possesses great skills in advertising, sales promotion, and online selling, and has values and mission that line up with your own. In reality, you need to prioritize certain abilities over others and make trade-offs to obtain a candidate who will do the best job, both now and in the long run.

Thinking in terms of priorities and trade-offs can be a challenge if you haven't been involved in search and selection before. You may find yourself overly focused on gaining the approval of others you respect—board members, team members, investors—and trying to make a hire that will please or impress them. As a result, you may hire someone with the most impressive credentials or who was recommended to you by one of your investors. This prevents you from assessing trade-offs and priorities objectively. For instance, let's say you're hiring for a leadership position, but this leader will also be an integral part of a team. What's more important: the ability to delegate versus the ability to contribute to the team dynamic? Similarly, you may have a list of competencies for the position, but which ones are more important than others? And what if a candidate seems to value the same norms as you do and her goals dovetail with the company's direction, but she lacks some prioritized skills?

Being able to weigh all these factors as you move through the recruiting process can make the difference between a great hire and good one.

Including Too Many People on the Evaluation and Selection Committee

This is a common beginner mistake, made with the best of intentions. You founded a startup and everyone is relatively new to the business. You're worried about recruiting, and so you create a committee consisting of investors, board members, and consultants to help you make key hires. The problem: Too many cooks spoil the broth. You'll end up with too many candidates and too many arguments over who is the right candidate. Instead, keep the number of people involved to yourself and up to three others to advise you. Be sure to select for your interview committee people who are adept at both selling and assessing against your Blueprint. In this way, you'll get a diversity of ideas but not a paralyzing and overwhelming amount.

Taking a "Blind" Recommendation

You hire someone based on the recommendation of someone you respect or who is in a position of power—a leader in your field, a consultant, an accomplished friend. They tell you, "Hire Joan, she is brilliant and worked for me at Company X and performed at a consistently high level. She's looking for a job, so make her an offer immediately so that no one else hires her before you."

Instead, ask yourself this question: Is this the right hire *for us*? These two little words change everything because then it's about a process to define and articulate the right profile, conceptual models, and methodology for securing the right hire for the company, the role, and the team. As much as you might trust and respect the person who is recommending a candidate, that person probably is unaware of your culture and mission—all the recommending person knows is that this individual performed well in a similar role in the past. What the recommender doesn't know—and you do after reading this book—is that fit is crucial. Joan can perform brilliantly for Company X but not for Company Y because of this factor.

THE BEST TEAM PLAYER

Speaking of teams, recruiting with this structure in mind is relatively new for many entrepreneurs. While teams have been the basic structural component in tech startups for quite a while, the same isn't true for other types of small businesses. They still retain a classic pyramid structure or some variation on it that relies on individual contributors for success. Entrepreneurs relish individual contributors, and rightly so, but teams are becoming the norm for all types of companies.

Recruiting for leadership or executive teams requires all the same principles I've discussed throughout the book. But beyond that, it helps to look for certain "types." I've found that the teams that perform best in entrepreneurial settings usually contain five distinct styles/abilities. Let's look at who these types are and how you can identify them during the recruiting process:

The Visionary

You may already have this person on your team—you. Typically, founders and CEOs are the ones with a grand idea and purpose. If you're a visionary for a railroad company, you're the one who discovers new, potentially profitable routes and decides if trains should go to these markets. It's possible, though, that you don't fulfill this role or that you need to hire someone with a fresh vision—someone who is more tied into new and emerging markets, for instance.

To find this individual, look for someone who can articulate a future for your company that is based on data, but who speaks about it with enthusiasm and conviction. People who can talk about all the great things they can do with your company are a dime a dozen; most leadership-level people talk a good game. But does this person support his vision with data—with a discussion of trends, market numbers, proven social media strategies? And does he talk from the heart, not just the head—is his vision something that he's passionate about?

The Operator

The analytical, detail-oriented operator is a necessary counterbalance to the visionary. This person is working behind the scenes, figuring out tactical execution to drive the unit economics of the business and achieve performance results. This person will ensure operational excellence and that the trains run on time.

To identify the operator, review the lessons of Chapter 10 on getting things done. Be alert for individuals who are detail oriented and task driven. They aren't the ones who spend the interview discussing theoretical business concepts or strategy; they aren't the visionaries. Instead, they relish budgeting and planning, figuring out solutions to knotty tactical problems. They don't mind working hard, and when you talk to them about all the tasks associated with the position, they respond positively.

The Engineer

A cousin of the operator, this person contributes to teams by filling the role of master crafter. In tech companies, this may mean heading the design team. But even in non-tech companies, this is a crucial role. Engineers design and build products or are responsible for creating and maintaining services.

During recruiting, it's relatively easy to identify engineers. Sometimes, they're obviously the ones who design the software or create the products. When it's not so obvious, search for people who love to build things. They like nothing better than sketching out ideas on napkins in restaurants or using whiteboards to sketch out their concepts. They create stuff—stuff that makes the company money and helps systems operate effectively.

The Dealmaker

Even the best and most innovative products don't sell themselves. You need a master dealmaker to lead distribution. This person has a knack for creative relationship building and can orchestrate the marketing and sales deals that fund your operation with the right pricing model.

Dealmakers may come from sales and marketing functions or they may be from other disciplines, but they are relationship builders and alliance makers. They're the ones vendors and customers call when they have problems, and they understand how to move people toward consensus, even when they are initially miles apart. During interviews, they like talking about the deals they've done and how they got done. The "how" is an element to seek; it shows that an individual relishes the process of dealmaking that gets results.

The Team Builder

This individual will have a high degree of emotional intelligence and a background in sales, recruiting, or other role interfacing with people. Individuals who facilitate teams can come from any function. What distinguishes them is an ability to bring the right people together in the right way and make sure they're doing the right things. In some tech companies, this individual is called the Chief People Officer, and it's an apt title. In a knowledge economy where data and insights are the differentiator, someone needs to take active responsibility for making sure that employees know how to work together to maximize their insights.

While recruiting, focus on candidates who can discuss teams from a deeply human perspective. In other words, they don't just use jargon to discuss team-building techniques but express their ideas about how to handle conflicts within teams, manage dominant personalities, and the like.

INVEST TIME, ENERGY, AND COMMITMENT

Not every entrepreneur wants to be involved in recruiting. If you've managed to avoid doing it in the past, you may be entering into the process reluctantly—either out of necessity (you have to hire someone fast) or because others are requesting your involvement. It's also possible that you want to be involved but there are many other things distracting you from this responsibility—you're dealing with a difficult customer or trying to fix a broken system.

Whatever the case, here's my advice: You can't be effective in recruiting if you do it halfway. If you just show up at the final interview to pick a candidate or make a hiring decision based on what your people have told you, you're not doing much good.

Even if you don't have much experience with recruiting or feel you're not very skilled at the tasks required, you need to be committed and involved through sourcing, screening, and securing. Never forget that you're the one who knows the company best—you're the one who is aware of the company's DNA and how you hope it evolves in the future. This knowledge will go a long way toward hiring the right person; it will go a long way even if you think you're a lousy interviewer or aren't that perceptive about people or lack the patience to review a long list of candidates.

Have other people help you do the recruiting tasks you're not that great at or aren't interested in doing. But stay involved, contribute your ideas, and meet with finalists for key positions. Even if this is the very first hire you've ever made, this involvement will serve you and your company well.

CHAPTER 12

The Employee of the Future

Recruiting with an Eye Toward Emerging Trends

T he good news is that this is the greatest time in history to be an entrepreneur, and the better news is that in the near future, it's going to be even greater. Significant problems and opportunities face every country and business sector, and large organizations often struggle with these problems and opportunities. Agility and innovation are necessary, and entrepreneurs possess these qualities in spades.

At the same time, the entrepreneurial company is changing, as are the people who work there. As you've probably experienced, things are moving faster; growth rates are increasing; the employee population is skewing younger; funding is more available. These and other trends are picking up steam and in the coming years, they will have a profound effect on who you hire and how you hire.

By taking a close look at these trends and their effects on entrepreneurs, we can see how they can and should impact your recruiting practices.

FOUR KEY TRENDS

It's not that the rules of entrepreneurial recruiting are going to change—in fact, everything I've written up to this point will be as valid five years from now as it is today—but that you'll need to keep other factors in mind as you recruit. To help you do so, let's look at the four most significant trends for entrepreneurs:

Creative Destruction

This term, originally attributed to economist Joseph Schumpeter a hundred years ago, means that innovation kills old models in order to usher in new ones. Schumpeter was referring to the death and birth cycle of industries caused by technological innovation. Today, it translates into the death and birth cycle of products and services—a cycle that is occurring faster and faster. The innovative cell phone from five years ago seems hopelessly old-fashioned today; no doubt, the creative destruction of our current smartphones will make them seem just as old fashioned in two or three years.

This trend affects recruiting in many ways, but one of them is the mindset of your workforce. Years ago, my parents assumed they could work at one company for thirty years and then retire with a pension. Obviously, that attitude has shifted. The liquidity in the labor market is increasing rapidly, so people join companies assuming that they may not be there for long. You need to recruit with a sense of what will keep a valued employee in place for more than a year or two. It's not going to be salary or perks or titles. It will be mission and values. Again, this is my mantra, and it should be yours: Find highly qualified employees who share your vision and beliefs about work, and they are likely to stay with you for the long term, or at least help you achieve your longer term goals.

Startups as Express Lanes to Learning and Growth

New entrepreneurial companies, especially in the tech sector, are flourishing. More money from venture capital, angel investors, and other sources is flowing toward great ideas than ever before. As beneficial a trend as this is for entrepreneurs with great ideas, it also comes with a hidden people cost. The drive to learn and grow requires employees who want to acquire new skills and knowledge and reach higher performance levels. When you're recruiting, you need to identify candidates who aren't simply content to do a job competently—even at a high level of competence. They must have a thirst for knowledge, be willing to endure a measure of discomfort as they try to master new skills and projects, and possess the motivation to become better managers and leaders.

Fragmentation of Attention Spans

Social media is a catalyst of this trend. Many people have difficulty sticking to one activity or even one project for long without their attention drifting to the notifications on their screens. This is a problem since focus is crucial to solving complex problems and coming up with innovative solutions. Entrepreneurial leaders need to be able to engage and motivate their people to focus—to concentrate with commitment and energy on their tasks. Therefore, they must recruit with an eye toward "engageability." Is a candidate someone who fidgets during interviews and who can't stay on topic? Or is this someone who has a laser-like focus and stays on point during a conversation?

The Rise of the Millennials

More twenty-six-year-olds exist in the United States than any other age, and by 2025, 75 percent of the workforce will be Millennials. As per the earlier point, this group often has more opportunities than ever before to fragment their attention spans and focus. Entrepreneurs, therefore, need to be especially alert to the ability of Millennial candidates to concentrate. Startups attract Millennials more than just about any other business, so founders must look beyond technological brilliance (which Millennials often possess in abundance) and look for employees who can focus and do deep work.

ONE TREND TO TAKE WITH A GRAIN OF SALT

At some point in the future, recruiting will be completely automated. I've heard a number of people make this suggestion, and I understand why they make it. Many entrepreneurs have used technology to spread the news of a job opening and search for potential candidates. It may seem logical to make the leap that in the future, new software will help them find exactly the right candidate both for a given position and a given company, that they will be able to plug all the job data in and find a candidate match.

What they're forgetting is that recruiting is the most human of business functions. Yes, technology can help generate a big list of candidates. But I defy anyone to make the argument that a piece of software can discern nuances of personality or depth of beliefs. Software may help you find a candidate who has all the right financial skills and experience to be your CFO, but it won't tell you if she'll fit into your culture; if her values and mission align with your own; if her more intangible qualities as a leader and a manager mesh with the people she'll be managing and leading. Assessing and selecting candidates is much more art than science, and technology hasn't yet reached the point where it's particularly good at the art part of the equation.

Speaking of CFOs and the financial department, you would think that this would be the first area where people would be replaced by machines, since the function is all about numbers. In fact, the typical financial department in an entrepreneurial company has at least as many employees today as it did ten years ago. While this function is far more dependent on technology tools than in the past, people still need to do a lot of the higher level, more abstract work—such as assessing the implications of the numbers and working with other functions to prioritize budgetary requests.

In the next few years, I anticipate that recruiting will add a variety of technological tools to facilitate higher level, more abstract tasks, especially for the screening and securing functions. At the very least, these tools will provide entrepreneurs with greater insights about each candidate's social media activities and web searches. At the most basic level, they will be able to discover if a potential candidate has done searches about his position salary, indicating that he may be unhappy with what he's receiving and is interested in moving elsewhere; or that he's visited sites providing career advice or how to deal with difficult bosses. On a more sophisticated level, technology might help us craft a deeper profile of a candidate. It might reveal that a given individual wrote a blog about the need for greater transparency in organizational communication or is active on sites that are involved in a philanthropic activity or participates in online forums about mentoring.

As useful as this technology will be for obtaining a clearer picture of who an individual candidate is, recruiting still boils down to a one-on-one process, especially when hiring for a senior leadership position or other key slot. There is no substitute for a genuine smile, understanding a person's deep motivations, and having a direct conversation with candidates and engaging in dialogues that reveal who these candidates are beyond what their actions—both in former jobs and online—suggest. What's more, the best target candidates will still need to be courted. The importance of properly *evaluating* potential hires is as high as *engaging* potential hires. But you must first *recruit* candidates into your hiring process before you can evaluate them.

RECRUITING IN A GROWING COMPANY

As you're no doubt aware, startups are everywhere. If possible, they will be even more ubiquitous in the coming years. Whether you're launching a new app from your home or an alternative energy business from an old-fashioned brick-and-mortar office, you're probably aiming for rapid growth—almost a necessity in a hyper-competitive marketplace. Fast growth will affect your recruiting efforts. More specifically, here are the six common phases of startup growth from a revenue perspective:

- $0 to $10 million in revenues
- $10 million to $25 million in revenues
- $25 million to $125 million in revenues
- $125 million to $375 million in revenues
- $375 million to $1 billion in revenues
- $1 billion plus in revenues

Think about these growth stages versus how companies used to grow much more slowly, often stabilizing in one of those growth categories and staying there. Back then, you could hire people for a stable stage and be reasonably assured that you wouldn't grow out of it for a number of years. Today, startups sometimes move through these revenue stages with surprising speed. As a result, they need to change their recruiting priorities.

In the beginning, startups need pioneers and missionaries. As the company matures, they require diplomats and politicians. Early on, startups need employees who can endure a financially brutal environment—they need people with guts and grit to get through the first and even the second stage. They also need dreamers, innovators, people who are believers and evangelists.

With growth, though, requirements shift. Companies need team builders and leaders, individuals who can help facilitate consensus and who can help others learn and grow. The more mature a company becomes, the greater the need for systems and processes, policies and procedures. I'm not saying companies should hire bureaucrats, but without structure and culture, mature companies will struggle.

If you're running a growing startup, you must adopt a continuous recruitment mentality. That's because employees generally don't stay engaged beyond two growth stages. They become disillusioned with the company's new direction: "It's not like it was around here when I joined" is a typical comment. Other people leave because as the company has grown, they have become more marketable; they receive offers from other startups that want them to help replicate this growth.

As a leader, therefore, be prepared to adapt your recruiting as people come and go (because you can be sure they will come and go). This means:

- In early growth stages, seek employees who relish flying by the seat of their pants; who are comfortable working without much structure; who are fiercely independent; who resonate strongly to the business you've created.
- In middle growth stages, look for people who want to build something, who want to be part of a company that is making a difference; who are capable of transitioning from being independent contributors to working on teams; who are interested in learning and growing in their careers.
- In the later stages, identify candidates who are adept at compromise and consensus building; who understand the nature of teamwork and function effectively leading or being part of teams; who want to put down roots in a company rather than hit the jackpot and run.

Obviously, this advice is generalized for different growth stages and who you hire depends on all the factors we've discussed previously. But you need to be prepared to do a lot more recruiting in the future, and to recruit with an eye toward the growth stage in which you find your company.

RECRUITING GROWTH MINDSET PEOPLE

If you have a growing company, you need people who possess a growth mindset. No matter what stage your company is at, these individuals resonate with enterprises and cultures where getting bigger and better are priorities. Growth is already a common goal for startups and many entrepreneurial ventures, but in the next five or ten years, it will become an imperative. Think about how your business and industry are changing. It's no longer possible for even small, out-of-the-way companies to rest on their laurels. No one can hide from global competition, the quick commoditization of innovative products, and escalating costs. The Internet makes new and old competitors all over the world immediately aware of your success, and you can expect someone to challenge you and try to take away some of your customers. As a result, you need to improve your strategy continuously, to be agile, to be creative, to take risks.

Employees who are content to remain in place, who settle for "good enough," who refuse to work harder than the norm, who prefer to do the same thing over and over rather than try something new—these are individuals who you don't want to recruit for your growing company in the coming years. They will make it difficult to be sufficiently flexible, innovative, and change-oriented to capitalize on all the abundant opportunities that exist.

In 2005, author Daniel Pink wrote a book titled, *A Whole New Brain: Why Right Brainers Will Rule the Future.* Though published quite a while ago, its lesson is still relevant—perhaps even more relevant today and in the next decade than it was when published. (This was a book ahead of its time.) Pink's premise is that we are moving from a time of left brain thinkers (analytical, detail-oriented, logical) to right brain ones (empathic, collaborative, story-centric). Other thought leaders have echoed Pink's points, but they are especially relevant to entrepreneurs.

One of the major errors neophyte entrepreneurs make is hiring for technical chops. They are so focused on hiring people with the best skills that they ignore or discount other qualities such as empathy, collaboration, and so on. In the past, they may have been able to get away with this error, but not in the future. They will see their best and brightest people deserting in droves because the company is growing and changing—they haven't affixed employees to the organizational essence by making sure they recruited individuals whose values and beliefs mirror their own. Or, they discover that their highly skilled workforce cannot work productively in teams (though they are excellent individual contributors).

Perhaps this is an oversimplification, but at some point in the future, there will only be two types of entrepreneurial companies—those that grow and those that die. The vast middle ground of companies that make modest, consistent profits year after year will become fewer and fewer.

If you are a company that is on the path of continuous growth, you have to recruit people with sales maven Zig Ziglar's advice in mind: "Your attitude, not your aptitude, will determine your altitude." Increasingly, technology in the form of artificial intelligence, machine learning, and other tools will provide a lot of the aptitude entrepreneurs require. What companies do with this aptitude depends on their people—on their ability to innovate, work together, take risks, take on stretch assignments, and so on.

Candidates with these growth mindsets don't accept jobs only because you've offered them the best salary. Though money is important, so too is their trust in what you're trying to accomplish and an affiliation with your values and goals. During the recruiting process, you build that trust and affiliation by focusing on purpose— theirs and yours.

PURPOSEFUL RECRUITING

It really wasn't that long ago when most entrepreneurs recruited by placing a help wanted ad in newspapers listing a fax number for resumes. On Monday morning, the human resources person would come in and find hundreds of resumes in the fax machine (assuming the HR person remembered to load it with paper and change the ink cartridge). Based on the resumes alone, HR would decide who to interview for the job; sometimes deciding that only half of the stack was worth looking at and that "luck" would play a role in who got interviewed.

We've come a long way in the past few years. We understand that with some additional work, you can know the whole person—not just where they work and what skills they've acquired. Interviews have become a crucial part of the process, in large part because they provide three-dimensional data that can be obtained nowhere else. This is the only way to know what makes a candidate tick.

More than ever before, we need to know what makes her tick. Now and in the years ahead, we need to dig deeper into who candidates are and how they will fit with a given company. It doesn't take a seer to predict that people more than products, services, and strategies will make the difference in the years ahead. There is so much parity in just about every product category that it's no longer who is first to market or who has the highest quality product or who has the best social media strategy.

It's about the people who execute that strategy. More specifically, it's about filling your company with people whose beliefs, goals, and vision add momentum to yours. I've emphasized this point so much throughout the book because I know the reflexive skepticism of pragmatic entrepreneurs. "I want to hire someone who can balance the damn books" or "I need to fill this position with the best programmer on the planet." When you're hungry for competency, it's easy to overlook values.

But competency will only get you so far in a world where all your competitors are competent. To gain a true competitive edge in a world where skilled people are ubiquitous, you need to find people with purpose—especially people whose purpose matches yours. That will not only provide you with a longer-term employee but with someone who works harder, faster, more productively, and more creatively. Mission-to-mission alignment creates exponential value for a company.

So recruit with purpose, today and in the foreseeable future. Don't wing it; recruit with a process to avoid hiring someone just because he "seems right." Purpose means methodology, and this book offers a method that has been proven to be effective time and again.

And recruit like an entrepreneurial leader. The most successful startup leaders—people I know and have worked with (and who are mentioned in these pages)—focused their recruiting efforts on core values alignment. They inspired and engaged their new hires based on this alignment. As a result, they brought in people who performed better than at any point in their careers, regardless of how their previous performance might have been.

You have all the knowledge you need to recruit in this way. And the knowledge you don't have you can acquire with ease (visit HireSmartFromTheStart.com for resources that will help you build your recruiting expertise). But to recruit at a high level, you really need to make a commitment—a commitment to align your workforce with your vision for and values of the business.

In one of the greatest motivational speeches ever made, Earl Nightingale quotes the psychologist and philosopher William James: "We need only in cold blood act as if the thing in question were real, and it . . . will become so knit with habit and emotion that our interests in it will be those which characterize belief."

James was suggesting that if you set a singular goal as your guiding star, your thoughts and habits will bend to it, and your mind will work toward it in ways you don't even consciously realize. In this way, you'll focus on this goal and figure out a way to make it a reality. Do this and you can facilitate self-transformation in the lives of the people you recruit, manage, and lead as well as in your own life.

Let your overarching purpose become a guiding star for your company. Then recruit people who can see that star just as clearly as you do. Find the talent who can navigate by its light.

If you do, you'll be amazed at how many candidates you select exceed even your most optimistic expectations. It all boils down to making the right match, and when you do, your company's fortunes will soar. What's more, you will achieve your mission.

INDEX

abundance, age of, 22
accountability, 84, 187
achievement in life, 94
action, translating values into, 194–196
agility, 179–180
alignment, 23–25, 34
amateurish approach, 72
Amazon, culture, 16
ambition, 131–132
anger, 118
Apple, 16
Arena quadrant (Johari Window), 109
arrogance, 182
attention span, fragmentation of, 219–220
authenticity, 102, 137–138
authority, lack of, 188
automation of recruiting, 220–222

Babinec, Martin, 14, 83
Ballmer, Steve, xii
Belbin, Meredith, 147
best hiring practices, mission and values and, 96

blind recommendation, 211
Blind Spot quadrant (Johari Window), 108, 109
vs. Mask, 40–43, 112–114
blueprint for tracking potential fit, 96–99, 172–173
board members, 169–170
Bock, Lazlo, *Work Rules*, 34
body language, 113
bragging, vs. humility, 113
business schools, entrepreneurial training, 22

camaraderie, 197
candidates
90-day plan from, 204
assessing perception of, 105
availability of multiple, 64–65
best already has better job, 79–80
blueprint for tracking potential fit, 96–99, 172–173
communication with, 34
discerning compatible beliefs and goals, 31
disrupting thinking, 157–158

candidates *(cont.)*
  diversity in, 63
  drivers for, 129–147
  failure to sell company to top
    level, 58–59
  hiring those who know more,
    62
  lack of internal, 56
  listening to, 206
  perfect, 209–210
  person behind, 106–111
  perspective, 201
  pitching company to, 62
  probing the depths, 142–147
  questions for, 44
  screening for red flags,
    115–119
  stories of, 121
catering, 76
certainty, creating, 158–159
change
  in entrepreneurial
    environment, 11
  impact on values or mission,
    103–104
  in recruiting, 12
character, 123
children, 155
clones, 170
  of entrepreneurs, 101–102
  hiring, 59–60
closing strategy, 204, 205–208
CNN, 21
cognitive ability, 147
collaborative intelligence, 18
Collins, Jim, 166
  Good to Great, 124
  Level 5 leadership, 124–125

commitment, ix
communication
  with candidate, 34
  pitching company to
    candidate, 62
compassion, 138–139
compensation, 203–204
competence, 39, 65
  settling for, 58
  stages, 160, 161
  vs. values, 227
competencies, focus on, 46
competitive advantage, 17
  people as, 2
confidence, 56
conflict, avoiding, 28
consensus, 24, 197
continuous growth, 226
contrasts, 74–75
control, vs. profits, 59, 169
core values, 83
  alignment, 228
  fit, 203
  maintaining, 48
costs, for key hires, 60
counteroffer, preempting,
    206–207
culture
  for checking candidate fit,
    99–101
  and company success, 14–15
  of harmony, Yahoo loss of, 47
  strategy and, 16–18
  synchronization with, 37
Cunningham, Keith, 37, 182

deadlines, 20–21
dealmaker, 214

decision process, 44
  of candidates, 45–46
  short-term and long-term, 167
Diamandis, Peter, 21
DISC personality test, 145
diversity, 102
  of ideas, 92
*Doing the Right Thing > Doing
  Things Right* (Suster), 195
dreams, 155, 159–160
drivers, for candidates, 129–147
Durant, Will, 48

eBay, 129–131
ego, offer and, 151
Einstein, Albert, 104
empathy, 156
employees, misalignment, 167
engineer, 213
Enron, 43
enthusiasm, ix, x, 159
  raising level for candidate,
    202–203
entrepreneurial environment,
  change, 11
entrepreneurs
  involvement in recruiting, 68,
    215
  lies to selves, 57
  overcoming obstacles, x
  responsibility for success, 15
  traits, 12
Epictetus, 38
Epstein, Theo, 36
errors, margins for, 1–2
  decreasing, 25–26
ethics, 25

excellence, as driver, 134–135
execution, 185–197
  candidate types, 191–194
  factors affecting, 186–191
  focus on, 63
  resources for, 191
executive search, 3
exit interview, preparing
  candidate for, 201–202
expectations of candidate, 206
expenses, control, and hiring
  decisions, 166–167
experience, lack of, 187
extracting candidates, 4, 6, 67,
  149–164
  evangelical zeal for, 68–69
  tactics, 153–160

Facebook, 23
  culture, 16
false harmony, 197
fax machine, 226–227
financial department, 221
financing, 17
*Finding Allies, Building
  Alliances* (Leavitt), 18
firing, 78
first impression, 105–106, 110
fixed mindset, 125–126
focus, lack of, 76
founder's dilemma, 169
The Founder's Dilemmas
  (Wasserman), 59
Freedman, Daniel, 37
freedom, offer and, 151
friends, hiring choices and, 82
fun as priority, 57

future
  for candidates, mapping, 208
  employee of, 217–229
  projecting, 157
  visualizing, 160

Gates, Bill, xii
General Electric, 16
Generation Fund, 152
generosity of spirit, 138–139
Gladwell, Malcom, "The Talent
  Myth," 43
goals, xii, 56
  focus on, 228
Gokhale, Aditi Javeri, 156
Good to Great (Collins), 124
Google, 34–35
  culture, 16
Gore, Al, 152
greatness, *see* myth of greatness
Grousbeck, Irving, 55–56, 69,
  77, 151, 166
growth
  vs. maintenance, 5
  potential of candidate,
    189–190
  startups and, 219
growth imperative, 26–27
growth mindset, 125–126
  and recruiting, 224–226

*The Hard Thing About Hard
  Things* (Horowitz), 13
hard work, 141–142
Harvard Business Review, 37
Haze, Butch, 36
helping others, as driver, 133
Herrmann Brain Dominance

Instrument (HBDI), 147
hiding information, 108
high-growth startups, criteria,
  4–5
high-level hires, 165–183
Hill, Napoleon, *Think and Grow
  Rich*, 18
hiring
  best practices, 96
  common rookie mistakes,
    208–211
  counteracting Greatness
    Myth effects on, 63–65
  first time, 199–215
  high-level, 165–183
  instincts in, 76–78
  by seat of pants, 1–2
  speed of, 171–173
  see also mistakes in hiring
Hogan Personality Inventory
  (HPI), 145–146
Hogshead, Sally, 146
honesty
  of candidates, 120
  and certainty, 159
Hootsuite, 93–94
Horowitz, Ben, *The Hard Thing
  About Hard Things*, 13
HotJobs.com, 3–4, 47, 131
How the World Sees You
  Assessment, 146
hubris, vs. humility, 41
human resources
  and hiring, 32–33
  perspective on, 13
humility, 136–137, 181–183
  vs. bragging, 113
  vs. hubris, 41

Iceberg/Honne Model, 142–143
ideas, creating diversity, 23
impact, offer and, 151
impatience, 60
implementation, *see* execution
impulsive hiring, 172
individualism, 28
informal exchanges, 138
information, hiding, 108
innovation, 7, 218
Instagram, 24
instincts, 170, 209
    in businessman, 70–71
    in hiring, 76–78
    vs. identification process for
        great hire, 59
    and mistakes, 1
intellectual spark, 203
intelligence, outlooks on,
    125–126
Internet advertising, 5–6
interviews, 227
    creating safe environment,
        120–122
    time for, 80–82
investments, return on, 20
Ironman Executive Challenge,
    134–135

James, William, 228
Jet.com, 78
job-seekers, passive, 35
Johari Window, 107–109
    Blind Spot vs. Masks, 112–114
Johnson, Steve, 93–94, 189
Johnson & Johnson, 16
judgments, 117
Jung, Carl, 145

Kahneman, Daniel, *Thinking
    Fast and Slow*, 1
Kasem, Casey, 171
Kellner, Peter, 152
knowledge, lack of, 187
knowledge economy, 7
Kolbe Assessments, 146

labor market, liquidity, 218
Ladders.com, 4
laissez faire approach, avoiding,
    69–71
Landsman, Liza, 78, 92, 189
leaders
    hiring, 165–183
    recruiting by, 32–36, 84
learning, 126
    from candidates, 62
    hunger for, 180–181
    potential of candidate,
        189–190
    startups and, 219
learning deficit, 109
Leavitt, Michael, *Finding Allies,
    Building Alliances*, 18
left brain thinkers, 225
legacy, as driver, 133–134
limited perspective, 54–57
listening
    to candidates, 206
    deeply, 156
lone wolves, 118

maintenance
    vs. growth, 5
    as strategy, 26–27
managers, hiring, 165–183
margins for error, 1–2

market analysis, 203–204
Marston, William Moulton, 145
Mask quadrant (Johari
    Window), 108, 110–111
  vs. Blind Spot, 112–114
masks, 114
  vs. blind spots, 40–43
  of Political Beasts, 116–117
  of Wallpapers, 119
Maslow, Abraham, hierarchy of
    needs, 123–124, 150
McKinsey Consulting Group,
    43
me-first people, 118
mentoring skills, 33
Microsoft, ix
mission, 38
  communicating for company,
    xii
  connecting personal mission
    with, 159–160
  definition of term, 88
  and extracting candidate, 154
  impact of change, 103–104
  mapping candidates,' 129–147
  motivation from, 190
  shared, 24, 55
mission mapping, 87–104
mistakes in hiring, xi, 51–66, 78
  avoiding biggest, 169–171
  instincts and, 1
  in recruiting caused by
    myths, 58–60
  refusing to admit, 115
modus operandi (MO), 146
money, as driver, 132–133
Moore, Gordon, 11
Moore's Law, 11

motivation
  intrinsic or extrinsic, 190
  lack of, 187–188
motivators, 44–45
  personal, 156
  for zeal and seal, 71–72
Movable Ink, 30–32, 133
Myers-Brigg Type Indicator
    (MBTI) Personality
    Inventory, 145
Myth of Greatness, 52, 56–57
  and candidate choice, 65
  counteracting effects on
    hiring, 63–65
  example, 52–53
  mistakes, 59–60
Myth of Smallness, 52
  and candidate choice, 65
  example, 53–54
  mistakes, 58–59
myths
  counteracting, 60–65
  examples, 52–54
  real option for, 65–66
  recruiting mistakes caused by,
    58–60

name-dropping, 116
Navy SEAL teams, 70
negativity, 78, 140
networking, 55
Nightingale, Earl, 228
Northwestern University, 22

offer, 38–39
  assessing level of, 150–153
  delivering with impact,
    207–208

openness, 139–140
operator, as team member, 213
opinions, freedom to share, 122
optimism, 140

passion, 159
passive approach to recruiting, 75
passive job-seekers, 35
Peddell, Louise, 31–32
people, as priority, vs. technology, 3
perception
   negative or positive, 21–22
   and reality, 105–127
perfect candidate, 209–210
performance, pressure for, 20
personal connection, 201
personal information, 154–156
personal mission statement, 89, 93–96
   connecting with organizational, 159–160
   examples, 94–95
personal style, 63
personality traits, linking to values, 96–99
perspective
   assessing, 12–15
   limited, 54–57
Pink, Daniel, *A Whole New Brain*, 225
Political Beasts, 116–117
posers/pretenders, 115–116
positive attitude, 140–141
pride, excessive, 115
Princeton Review, 22
priorities, 210

hiring right employees as, 25–28
people vs. technology, 3
talent selection as, 67
proactive leaders, 34
Procter & Gamble, 43
product life cycle, 218
productivity, 185–197
   achieving, 196–197
professional employer organizations (PEOs), 83
professional virtues, 135–142
profits, vs. control, 59, 169
promoting from within, 176–177
Prothero, Stephen, 126
purpose, 73
   recruiting with, 228

qualities, required, 178–183
   agility, 179–180
   humility, 181–183
   hunger for learning, 180–181
questions
   for candidates, 44
   for depth, 144

rapid growth, recruiting and, 19–20
recruiting
   automation of, 220–222
   change, 12
   checklist, 202–204
   growth in, 222–224
   investing time, energy, and commitment, 215
   involving others in, 163–164
   by leaders, 32–36

recruiting *(cont.)*
mistakes caused by myths,
58–60
as one-on-one process, 222
purposeful, 226–229
rapid growth and, 19–20
slowing down, 29–49
recruiting consciousness, 34
recruiting levels, 5–6
level 2, 19
level 3, 65
recruitment firms, 82–83
choosing, 84–85
references, 111
referrals and networking, 6
religion, 126
resources, 228
responsibility, for success, 15
resumes, 34, 226–227
return on investments, 20
reward and recognition system,
100–101
Richmond Global, 152
right brain thinkers, 225
risk, acknowledging, 182
Rocket Fuel (Wickman and
Winters), 193
Room to Read, ix, xi

Salesforce, culture, 16
Schumpeter, Joseph, 218
screening stage, 200
searching
for high-level people, 123–126
taking time for, 60
securing stage, 200
selection committee, size of,
210–211

self-actualization, 152
self-awareness, 114
Semmelbauer, Thilo, 133,
182–183
services life cycle, 218
Shackleton, Ernest, 38–39
Sharma, Vivek, 30–32
shortcuts, and lawsuit exposure,
63
Shutterstock, 134, 161–163
Sinek, Simon, *Start with Why*,
73, 74
small team leader, finding,
174–175
smallness, *see* Myth of
Smallness
Smart, Bradford, *Topgrading*, 67
social media, 26
and values, 34
Song, Mary Lou, 36, 129–131
sourcing stage, 200
spark, ix
speed, 21
in execution, 7
of hiring, 171–173
need for, 27–28
Standard & Poor's, 152
stars, recruiting, 36–40
Start with Why (Sinek), 73, 74
startups
criteria for high-growth, 4–5
employees needed, 223
learning and growth, 219
phases of growth, 222–223
proliferation of, 22
stories, of candidates, 121
strategy, priorities, 38
success, responsibility for, 15

Sullivan, Dan, 18
Suster, Mark, *Doing the Right Thing > Doing Things Right*, 195

talent, 37
  as priority, 67
  taking advantage of, 7
talent facilitators, 35
team builder, 214–215
teams, 28
  collaboration in, 33
  player types, 211–215
  value consistency, 17
technical skills, 189, 220–222
  hiring for, 225
  as priority, vs. people, 3
  as priority, vs. value, 175–176
technology, 43
  speed, 11
Teed, Rick, 36
Think and Grow Rich (Hill), 18
thinking, left brain vs. right, 225
Thinking Fast and Slow (Kahneman), Kahneman, Daniel, 1
top candidates, failure to sell company to, 58–59
Topgrading (Smart), 67
trade-offs, 209
training, 83
  for entrepreneurs, 22
  internal candidates, 177
transparency, 98–99, 139–140
trends, 217–229
  attention span fragmentation, 219–220

creative destruction, 218–219
  millennials, 220
  startups, and learning and growth, 219
TriNet, 14, 83
troublemakers, 117
trust, in process vs. instincts, 77
TSNL (Take Stuff to Next Level) potential, 24, 49
TTI Success Insights, 146

underbudgeting for key position, 58
"unknown potential" factor, 108–109
upside potential, recruiting for, 56
upward mobility, 132

value of great hire
  calculating, 60–65
  of true believers, 72
values, 14
  of candidates, 39–40, 44
  vs. competence, 227
  definition of term, 88
  and extracting candidate, 154
  identifying, 91–93
  impact of change, 103–104
  individual vs. high-level core, 174
  linking personality traits to, 96–99
  maintaining company's, 46–49
  mapping, 87–104
  mapping candidates,' 129–147
  motivation from, 190

values *(cont.)*
  as priority, vs. technical skills,
    175–176
  ranking, 92–93
  refocusing attention on,
    65–66
  searching for, 31
  translating into action,
    194–196
vision, 5, 39
  communicating, 62
  questions to determine, 89–90
  sharing, 20, 80
visionary, as team member, 212

Wallflowers, 119
Wal-Mart, 43
Wasserman, Noam, 169
  The Founder's Dilemmas, 59
Watson-Glaser Critical
    Thinking Appraisal, 146
weakness, candidate response
    to, 112
Weight Watchers, 133–134,
    182–183
Welch, Jack, 34
A Whole New Brain (Pink), 225
why, focus on, 73–74
Wickman, Gino, *Rocket Fuel*,
    193
Winters, Mark C., *Rocket Fuel*,
    193
Wonderlic, 147
work ethic, xii
Work Rules (Bock), 34
world, vision to improve, 89–90

Yahoo, 47–48
You See/I Don't See quadrant
    (Johari Window), 108
You See/I See quadrant (Johari
    Window), 107

zeal-and-seal, 74
  capitalizing on others, 82–85
  motivators for, 71–72
Ziglar, Zig, 226